FOREWO

The Newark Patriotic Fund began i ... a young Lance Corporal in the Grenadier Guards was injured in Afghanistan. He lost a leg and died a couple of times on his way back to the UK. The MOD were doing all they could for him, however, very little was being done for his next of kin, his mum and dad. They couldn't afford to keep going down to Selly Oak in Birmingham, so a group of locals got together and paid so that his mother could be with him. His father's company weren't being cooperative with regard to giving him time off to see his son, so pressure was applied on them and they gave him the time he needed.

From that moment, we realised that there was a greater need to help the families of our injured service personnel, so we formed the fund and started to raise much needed money. The fund now also supports our injured service personnel, people with "hidden wounds" like PTSD, as well as physical injuries, and their families. We bring a wraparound service to the whole of the family, supporting them with housing issues, CV writing and job applications, and we also support them with financial management.

Most of all, we are there as a safety net and to listen. In 2014, we became a charity and are a well established go-to organisation for other groups and authorities.

You will be pleased to know that the Lance Corporal is now married with children and doing very well.

That's what the Newark Patriotic Fund is all about.

~Keith Girling
Founder Member
Chairman of Trustees

PREFACE

Everyone has a story. Each story is utterly unique to the person telling it. It's important we hear from the people who live these stories, from those who are often voiceless in a world filled with the noise of less important matters. If we stop and take the time to read, to listen, and to understand, we gain insight into the world beyond our personal frontiers. We can learn from people's experiences and develop empathy. Through empathy we become mindful of the struggles of others, and show that they are both seen and heard. By reading individual stories from those who have been where we can not conceive, we become better people.

For Global Wordsmiths, it was important not only that we bring you stories from those who have served, but that we also bring you the words of those who support and love them. The stories of partners, parents and children who are also affected by their military lives, are so often unheard, but they are no less important, no less emotional. This project was as much about hearing the stories as it was helping people to tell them.

Thank you to each and every writer who found the courage to put their story down on paper for others to read. I hope, through reading one another's stories, you realise that you are all, truly, heroes.

~Victoria Villasenor, Ed.

CONTENTS

MY SON
BY MARGARET WRIGHT

I look at this young man, so tall and so strong,
And I do have to wonder whatever went wrong?
Each job he did, he gave it his all,
And no-one could know how far he would fall.
His comrades-in-arms, who fought overseas,
Many were crippled with wounds you could see.
But some, like this man, still whole to the eye,
Are crippled inside and it just makes me cry.
The memories they hold still eat at them so,
The dreams that they suffer will not let them go.
The problems they deal with remain sight unseen,
When they wake in the morning, who knows where they've been.
They have no injuries others can see,
No missing limbs cut off at the knee.
Their families struggle to do what they can.
They just want to help this poor damaged man.
We all know the letters, and quote them off-hand,
And make our donations to that brother's band.
But no-one else knows how hard it can be,
For our soldiers who suffer with PTSD.

A Completed Dream and a New Path
By Alyson Trapp

I was sitting on the sofa with my family, waiting for the news to come on. The main story was about the Falkland War and the events that were taking place. I would watch with great interest, hoping to see my uncle, who was in the Royal Marines. I was only nine years old, but I would watch the aircraft leaving their ships, attacking the enemy, and over the days I would watch, fascinated by their role in the war.

After watching these aircraft, and a lot of thought, (for a nine year old, anyway), I decided I wanted to go into the military and fix aircraft. I would sit in my bedroom watching the jets fly past, not knowing what they were. So I started to read about military aircraft and their roles, and found out they were Tornados. I studied them and they became my favourite aircraft. It became my dream to work on them. I told my parents that I wanted to join the Royal Air Force, and they were very supportive. I continued to feel this way even when I went into secondary school, and one of my teachers who was also a career advisor, helped me out. He gathered loads of information about military job roles and how to apply. I also had a training guide to work to, which my mum did with me. It was hard and painful, but I wasn't going to give up.

I worked hard at school, knowing the GCSE's I needed to be an Aircraft Mechanic (Airframes). My parents also looked into the Air Cadets, so I could learn more about the Royal Air Force, and I joined at fifteen years old. I enjoyed learning the history and roles, they taught me how to shoot, drill, and even combat exercises which were a great laugh, attacking each other in the field, getting covered in muck, and trying to hide whilst escaping the enemy. They even let me carry on my fitness training whilst there. I would go and do my six mile jog, and come back to carry on with activities. Eventually, I did my exams in 1989 and passed the ones I needed to be an Aircraft Mechanic.

I was so excited, but I knew I still had a long way to go. My parents took me to the careers office in Nottingham and spoke to the Royal Air Force advisor, and filled in all the paper work. They booked me in for my aptitude test, which I passed, but sadly I failed on the mechanical section. I was so upset, but I could retake it in a year's time, and that meant I had to think what to do in the meantime. I decided to try YTS on car mechanics at college. I knew it would be hard, and being the only female on the course, the lads gave me a hard time, but I ignored them and studied hard. I even started getting higher marks than them, and they started to respect me.

After completing my first year of the car mechanics course, I sat the aptitude test again and passed, but then was told that I would have to wait another year to start as an Aircraft mechanic. I was fine with that, though, because I knew I was headed the right direction.

I went back to college and did my second year as a car mechanic, and carried on with my fitness training. I then received the letter stating my enlistment date, 25th June 1991, and it said a coach would pick recruits up at Newark station and take them to RAF Swinderby for six weeks basic training. My dream was coming true, the goal I'd had from the time I was nine years old finally in sight. I knew it would be tough, but I wasn't going to quit and remained strong. I had worked hard for years and wanted to make my parents proud.

In 1992, I had passed my basic training at RAF Swinderby and finished my seven month Aircraft Mechanic Course at RAF Halton. I was over the moon that all my training was finished, and my first posting was at RAF Lyneham, to work on the C130 Hercules doing minor servicing. The team were brilliant and I enjoyed my work. I had wanted this posting for a personal reason, too. My dad is a big fan of the Hercules aircraft, and I was going to make his dream come true, to thank them for all the support they'd given me through the years. I had learnt that the base had an opening day for family to come to see the base. There would be air displays as well, so my parents and my brother and sister came down. it was great to see them, and to see my dad's face light up when he could go on the Hercules and have a look around. I even took a picture of him standing in front of the Hercules with his thumbs up. My mum was also happy, as she saw her favourite aircraft, the Vulcan bomber, do an air display. We had loads of fun, but the best was to come. A family day included the opportunity to go up in a Hercules, and there was no way my dad was going to miss it! When they arrived they signed up, then headed outside and walked onto the Hercules. My dad's face lit up, he was so excited.

We were told to take our seats and get ready for take-off. Then I started to feel ill, which my brother took great pleasure in making fun of me for. The flight over Wiltshire was great, then the Aircrew opened the ramp and door, which had a net up, and they allowed people onto the ramp to look out the rear, which my dad really loved. He really enjoyed the whole experience, and it was great to make my dad's dream come true. We even did it again the next year, but I stayed on the ground while my family went up.

I stayed at RAF Lyneham until 1995, when, due to a sad family event at home, I was posted to RAF Cottesmore on Tornados. These were the same Tornados that used to fly over my house when I was a kid. I couldn't believe it, I had achieved my dream and practically come full circle. I was so happy, and I loved working on them. I worked on the Tornados for just over four years, then went on to the Aircraft Technician (Airframe) Course. I was posted back to RAF Cottesmore after my course and worked on the Harriers, which moved to the base.

This was my last posting, and due to having problems with my hands from working as a mechanic for so many years, I learnt that I could only do my fifteen year service, which ripped me apart, as I always wanted to do my twenty-one years.

Sadly, I left the Royal Air Force in June 2006, knowing I had to have surgery on my tendon in my right hand, and suffering with Carpal Tunnel Syndrome. I knew I had a tough journey ahead of me. I had surgery on my hand December 2006, but they decided not to do Carpal Tunnel Decompression, as it wasn't too serious. Over the months, though, both my hands started to get worse. I went from not being able to feel anything, to dropping things as my hands would go numb. The cold would make them ache terribly. I had to go back to the doctor and see what they could do. I was sent to a hand surgeon, and he was happy to operate. I had the first Carpal Tunnel Decompression operation on my left hand, then a month later on the right hand.

The operations failed.

I was unhappy, and knowing that a second operation had an even a smaller chance of repairing my hands, my world fell apart. My engineering days were over, and I slowly sank into depression. I couldn't cope with the pain, numbness, having to wear wrist supports at night, and having sleepless nights because of the pain. Everything I learned, from being a car mechanic to being an Aircraft Technician, was useless now. Slowly, I shut myself away, only going out to take my son to school and pick him up. The other parents made me feel like an outsider, as I was ex-military and I know some of them hated it, but I tried to ignore a lot of them. Over the years, I had more operations on my elbow and my right wrist, but I continued struggling and feeling helpless.

I had my family around me, but hardly any friends until I saw a newspaper article about The Newark Patriotic Fund. They helped injured service personnel, so I plucked up the courage and went to see what the Fund was about. It was fantastic. I slowly met other service veterans and started making new friends, and it was great to finally talk to people in the same situation. It was also good having the same banter, like being back in the military family, which most non-military people don't understand.

I still find it hard to come to terms with my injuries, and I still miss working on aircraft. I cry sometimes when I see the jets fly over. I can't even fix my own car, and having worked so hard over the years to achieve my dreams, now I feel useless. I now have to think about a new path with these bad hands, and I'm thinking maybe working with animals would be good, as I love my pets and animals in general. Knowing I'm restricted to what I'm able to do, and also having to cope with depression, it's not an easy task, but I know I have great friends and family to help me find my next career.

THE MAN I MARRIED
BY CAZ

I married the man I wanted to spend the rest of my life with on 3rd Dec 2005. The wedding day was perfect despite having only five weeks to plan and organise it. I was due to have our first child the following May, and we had just found out that John was due to deploy to Iraq the same time I was due. I was devastated. I had visions of going through the birth of our first child without him by my side. What if something went wrong? How would I get through it without him? I tried to put the other thoughts I had to the back of my mind, as I didn't want to contemplate my life without him, and him never seeing his little girl.

It was all a little sudden; it hadn't been planned that his battalion was going, so it was a real big rush to get the training done, which meant he was away a lot during the pregnancy and we were still unsure if he would still be in the country for the birth. The due date soon arrived; it was a beautiful girl and we chose the name Grace. John had been given five extra days at home so we could spend it as a family before he deployed on his four month tour. It was really upsetting saying goodbye and not knowing the next time I would hear his voice. We kept in touch by sending blueys (blue letters we could use and send free of charge). John would also call when he could, and I would send pictures of Grace every few days so he didn't miss anything.

I was staying with my mum and dad while John was away, and as soon as he was home we moved to Aldershot, to our first home as husband and wife. It was hard moving so far away from my family for the first time but I was also excited about the start of my new life as a wife and a mum.

Our house was nice and cosy, but soon after moving in John started training for a tour of Afghanistan. He was deploying in March 2007 and it meant he was away a lot. I began to feel like a single person on my own, and I started to miss being around my family, but Grace kept me busy. In November we found out I was expecting again and we were both over the moon. I was due at the end of July 2007, but with John's training being so intense and then him deploying, all I could think about was that I would be going through the whole pregnancy and birth by myself. I kept positive, though.

In March, we moved to a new three bedroom house. I loved it—I finally had a garden for Grace to play in, and the new house was big and roomy. Two days later, it was time for John to deploy again. I settled in and got to know the new neighbours, and also went home quite a lot to see my family. It was a lonely time and wasn't nice going to bed on my own, with the fear of not knowing if John was okay, knowing the door could be knocked on at any time with bad news. His battalion had set up a texting service to inform us of any incidents where someone had been injured in Afghanistan, so when we got these texts we knew that our loved ones could not contact us.

John had chosen a late R&R, a two week break back home with family, to rest and recuperate, so he could be home for the birth of Emily. I had been watching the news and seen the injured soldiers and the ones who never made it home. A close friend of ours had been seriously injured and it put into perspective the reality of what it was really like out there. The day John came home I hardly recognised the very thin, tired and aged looking person before me at the front door. He had a big smile on his face and I picked up Grace and reintroduced her to her daddy. We had a week together before I gave birth to our beautiful second daughter Emily, and despite John not having long with us again, we made the most of the short time we had. He got stuck in to being a dad.

While John was on leave, he saw the tragic news of a close friend that had been killed. He'd seen him only days before he came home. I didn't even know what to say. I could tell by looking at him that he was devastated, and I couldn't even begin to imagine what he was going through. John's flight back to Afghanistan had been delayed, which meant we had even more time together and that we could attend his friend's funeral. We travelled to Manchester to attend the funeral; it was a lovely ceremony and that day will stay with me for the rest of my life. It was such a tragic loss of a young man with a child of his own. We never really spoke about the funeral once we got home. John just wanted to spend as much time with the girls and not talk about anything else. In a way, I suppose he was protecting me from what he was really going through. I had my mum for support but often didn't say much about how I was feeling, because then it would feel even more real.

Four days later it was time for John to return to Afghanistan, and I didn't want to let him go. But I soon got back into a routine of being on my own, and the fear of terrible news. I became close to another army wife and we helped each other through what seemed like really long days.

John returned home at the end of October. I couldn't wait to collect him and bring him home, and Grace was excited in the back of the car as we pulled up. I got out to give him a massive hug, noting that he looked very tired and thin. But still, he had a huge smile on his face as he opened the car to give the girls a big kiss. It was such a relief to have him home, and we were soon settled into being a normal family again.

It was soon summer and we had some new neighbours. There were loads of BBQ's, laughs and memories, but it was short lived, as we had to move again. This time it was to Chertsey. I hated the place even before we moved. It was in the middle of nowhere and the houses were old and had been empty for years, but in August 2008 we moved into the new house. There were only thirty-three houses on the street and we were soon invited to a BBQ. I got to know some new people and make some new friends, and I thought that maybe the move wasn't so bad after all.

John went away to training again because he was going back to Afghanistan in September 2009. While living at the new house we had had some problems with our neighbours. They eventually got evicted and their house, and ours, was condemned. I was so relieved. We had lived next to them for six long months, and we'd had to seal Emily's bedroom window shut, as the windows were so bad and rotten, and the smell from next door's house would seep through. We also had rats in the garden.

Finally, we could move again.

We were moved onto the next street, and this house was lovely. It was really big and had a garage and a forest at the back of the garden. There were only twelve houses on this street. I soon got to know our new neighbours once again, and John was getting ready to deploy. He had summer leave before he had to go, and we made the most of it, making memories. The day had come to say goodbye and I drove him and a friend to Wellington Barracks in London, ready for another deployment back to Afghanistan. The drive back home through London was very teary. I hated saying goodbye and was beginning to really hate being on my own. My family and friends kept each other comforted and we all gave one another what support we could. This helped me get through some tough days, though sometimes I just liked to be left alone.

The girls were only two and three, so they didn't really understand what was going on, but they spoke to John on the phone and sent him pictures. They also helped pack parcels to send him.

The feeling of fear had returned, along with the sleepless nights. Not knowing if there would be a knock at the door and not knowing John was safe was awful. The text messages from his battalion seemed to be more frequent this time, and me and the other wives would text each other to check everything was okay. The days seemed to drag and before I knew it, it was Christmas. I went home to my parents, but it didn't feel right without John at home. We had presents wrapped up ready for him to open once he was home, and had sent a few things out to Afghanistan for him.

The day came for me to return home. A friend had gone home to spend Christmas with her family as well and we were both heading back to Chertsey on the same day. Just before I left, I had received a text from the battalion. The text message was always the same; it would say that there had been an incident in Afghanistan and next of kin had been informed. I hadn't heard from John, but was hoping to later in the day. I arrived back in Chertsey and text my friend to make sure she was home safe. She didn't reply, but phoned a couple of hours later and her voice was panicky. In my heart I knew there was something wrong with her husband, the friend I had taken to Wellington Barracks with John. He'd been injured, shot in the leg, but had complications and died several times before being made stable and flown home. All I wanted to do was hear John's voice and let him know how much I loved him. He phoned later that night, tired, and we spoke about our friend. I didn't want the phone call to end. I was upset, worried, and anxious all the time. I just wanted him home.

We were now well into January and the count down for John's R&R had begun. Our friend was home with his wife and starting his recovery. John came home on 10th February 2010. It was seven a.m. and the girls were excited, as they knew we were collecting him from Brize Norton. We arrived at the airport at eight thirty, and John was due to land at nine. I was in the waiting room, trying to get the girls to sit down, when the doors opened. The girls rushed over, looking for their dad, but all the soldiers looked the same, which confused them a little. As each man walked through the doors they smiled at the girls, who were eagerly waiting for their dad, who was the last man through.

It was amazing seeing other people reunited with their loved ones, and the girls and me rushed over to John, who scooped up both girls in his arms. They wouldn't leave his side once we were home. We went to visit family, and on Valentine's Day I'd booked a surprise meal for us and two friends. That day, I had received a text alert from the battalion. John was frustrated because he couldn't find out who it was. Then we did, and it wasn't good news. Tragically, yet another friend had lost his life. We decided to cancel the meal and instead went for a drink to mourn the loss of his and our friend's mate.

That night, I saw John in a way I'd never seen him before. He was devastated and didn't know how to control his emotions for the first time. I felt helpless and it was heart breaking. I never wanted him to return to Afghanistan. It soon came around though, and I was back to saying my goodbyes.

John was due to be back seven weeks after returning to Afghanistan, and I wished every day that time would speed up. The night before John came home, me and the girls made a welcome home banner. The girls loved doing it, they had paint everywhere, and John loved it as well. The doorbell rang and the girls rushed to the door and John was finally home.

Over the next few weeks I noticed that John was quite withdrawn. He was quiet in himself, not sleeping well and he was jumping at loud noises. He just got on with it though, and we never really spoke about the tours and what he had done or seen. I got used to not asking and just figured that he would talk when he wanted to. That summer was busy, almost like he was still on tour. He was away a lot on courses to further his career. That winter we moved back to Aldershot, as I'd had an operation on my shoulder and was unable to drive. In Chertsey you really needed to be able to drive. It was a relief moving back to Aldershot. Although I liked my house in Chertsey, I hated living there. I felt isolated, and hated having to drive everywhere, and I never really had a social life in Chertsey like I did in Aldershot.

The day we moved it was freezing, and two days before Christmas it snowed really heavy. The girls loved it; we all had massive snow ball fights and built snowmen. Grace was soon settled into her new school and Emily her nursery. John was enjoying working in Aldershot and not having to commute to London everyday like he had in Chertsey. It felt like a weight had been lifted and we had less pressure. I managed to get myself a little part time job that would keep me busy when John was away. It was great, as it also meant we had more money to do things as a family.

John went to Canada for four months to train, and although the girls were old enough to notice now, we simply spent the time counting down to when he came home. At least he wasn't in Afghanistan. I still worried a little, but I knew he was essentially safe out there.

When he got back, John started to train for the next tour of Afghanistan. I was already beginning to hate the thought of being on my own again; it's so hard being a family, but not being all together. John never seemed to be home. People think it's only a six month tour, but they forget that they need to train for six months before, so it ends up being almost a year without a loved one. We went away in March 2012 for a family holiday, which was great but seemed to fly by. The girls were now five and six, and had started to ask the odd question about John being away, but how do you explain it to children so young?

It was time to say goodbye again, and I was already overcome with the same old fears: not knowing when I'd speak to him again, and praying there wouldn't be the dreaded knock on the door. He gave the girls camo hats for their teddies, and told them to wave every time they see an airplane. We'd talked a bit about the new tour, and I knew John was uneasy about it.

When John called to check in, he said morale had been low, that in a month, not a single letter or parcel had been received. When he came home briefly, he didn't say much, other than morale had been low. When he came home off tour in October, he looked worn out, but glad to be home.

John seemed very quiet and easily annoyed. I put it down to him being tired and trying to settle back into normal life. But then it became clear something was wrong.

It was Thursday night and we went out with some friends. We all had a really good night. And then, after being at home for about an hour, something happened, and I found myself in an awful place. I'd woken up screaming. John was trying to strangle me, and I couldn't understand what he was saying. He was shouting things out, but I couldn't understand them. I managed to get him off me and got off the bed. Grace was standing in the doorway, and she'd turned the light on. I looked at John, and it was like I didn't know the man standing before me. He was still enraged and started to smash things in the bedroom. I was terrified, and worried for mine and the girls safety, so I grabbed the house phone and called the police. I couldn't believe what I was doing. The police arrived and took John away. I could see that there was something wrong with him, and he's been a different person since that last tour. The following day I had a meeting with the Battalion Welfare Officer. We talked about my concerns, and he suggested we shouldn't drink for a while. Later that day, John was released from the police station, and he called me to pick him up. I was nervous about seeing him again after what had happened. He said he couldn't remember a thing. My parents had travelled over to be with us and we spoke with them about what had happened.

I'd never seen John like that before; he wasn't sleeping, and when he did he had nightmares that woke us both up. He still wasn't talking to me about anything, and just said that he was fine. I spoke to a friend, and she said she had noticed that he seemed quieter, and not as sociable as he was before. I didn't know what I could do.

It was December, and the night of our Christmas Ball. We'd been looking forward to it and John seemed relaxed. We arrived with two friends and everyone looked smart in their mess dress and the women in their ball gowns. The marquee looked amazing. The food was served and the drinks were flowing; we all let our hair down. There was a bit of talk about the tour between the lads at the table, and the mood dipped slightly. Once we got home we talked to the friends that had looked after the girls, and out of nowhere John seemed to be that unknown man again. He was angry and couldn't control himself. I had to call the police again. There was something wrong with him and we couldn't pretend anymore.

My parents travelled to Aldershot again for support and over the next few days I had meetings again with the welfare team and a few other people. I raised my concerns again, and this time they seemed to be taking me seriously.

At the start of the New Year, John started to see a CPN every week and was given some medication to try and help him sleep. He didn't mention what he and his CPN talked about, so I was left wondering what they were saying, and then I started to panic. What if he wanted to leave me? I just kept thinking, at least he's getting some help. The girls asked questions and talked about what had happened. John was signed off work for three months. I was exhausted, and John was still restless, even with his medication, but he didn't have the energy to do anything.

Three months passed, and John no longer spoke to or saw anyone. His friends stopped texting and we no longer got invited to anything. Friends asked how he was if I saw them, but no one really understood what he was going through or what it was like to live with him. He had no energy to do anything, and we no longer went out as a family. He stopped playing with the girls and became very short tempered. It was like he was pushing us all away. Most people said that he should return to work, or mentioned that they had seen him and he looked fine. In the end I gave up explaining myself and the situation. This opened my eyes to who my true friends were. I think because we stopped doing people favours, we were no longer needed.

John was signed off for another six months while having treatment. He did a long course of EMDR, then they tried CBT (cognitive behavioural therapy), and he also did a course of anger management. In October 2013 they finally decided that because of his severe PTSD, he would be discharged from the military in October 2014. Once we knew he would be discharged we started to save some money for a deposit on a house, so we could move back home to be nearer to our families. It was a rough three to four months looking for a house. Three times we had offers accepted and the first two fell through, which was hard financially and mentally. It put a lot of pressure on us, and for some weeks we were split up from each other, staying with different family members. It made John feel useless. I began to wonder when we would get a break and just be happy.

Once we moved, the battalion only did the bare minimum that they legally had to, and since leaving he has heard nothing at all. It's quite upsetting that after thirteen years serving that regiment they've shown little interest in the soldiers that have mental scars. They haven't even done a courtesy follow up call to see how any of us are doing. I was disgusted, but not surprised, because I had learnt that this is how they treat their service men and women. It makes you question how anyone that leaves and has an illness manages to have a life outside the army.

When it was John's last day in the army, on 31st October 2014, I felt sorry for him. He had put so much into being the best soldier he could be, and we were all so proud of everything he had done. He now has to cope with every day as it comes. People know he was in the army and has PTSD, and don't really question us about it anymore. It's nice being home and having the support of our families, who are always there to support us. Every day is still a struggle, and the new fight is trying to get help through the NHS. They are very slow and not as helpful as they should be. A simple thing like changing medication has taken five months and he is still waiting. It's frustrating for John and myself. I still really don't know what he's going through, and I don't think I ever will.

I'm still busy looking after the girls and helping them manage with things and so far-so good, they are growing into lovely little girls, but I think the stress of everything is sometimes too much for them. John has changed from the man I married ten years ago. He's not as outgoing and we have to plan things in advance, knowing sometimes we may have to cancel them. I know to give him space if he needs it. I still find things difficult, as he doesn't like to let me in and let me know what he's feeling. I treasure the days we have when he's like his old self, and we have a laugh and a giggle together and just forget about things.

People will always say, 'you knew what you were getting into by marrying a soldier,' but my answer is...No, I didn't know. No one could ever be prepared for the heartache you go through, no one could ever tell you how little time you get to spend together. But one thing I do know is that I wouldn't change my life for anything. If anything, it's made me a stronger person. As long as the four of us have each other, we can get through anything. I would advise anyone finding themselves in a similar situation to seek help and continue to fight to get help for their loved ones. Don't give up, on them, or getting them the help they need.

EVERY DAY IS A GIFT
BY ASHLEY TOPHAM

I was born on the 4th July 1965, in Poole, Dorset. My father was in the Royal Air Force, so I spent the first sixteen years of my life travelling around the country, living on Air Force camps. From an early age, all I had wanted to do was to join the British Army. I was a bit of a lad at school, but I was a good sportsman, fit and of average intelligence, and believed the Army was the place for me.

I joined the British Army at the age of sixteen as a Junior Soldier, and it began the career I had always wanted. I was so pleased when the day finally arrived to start on my ultimate career path. I served for twenty-four years, achieving the rank of Warrant Officer Class One Regimental Sergeant Major, the top soldier in a British Army Regiment. I had a great career, and I had the chance to actually go to war, an opportunity not every soldier gets. I met some great people, who are great friends to this day. My Army career did not go smoothly all the time; my best claim to fame was when three of us skied over the East German boarder by mistake, at the height of the cold war. We were captured by the Russians and caused an international incident. Margaret Thatcher, the Prime Minister at the time, was involved in getting three of her soldiers out of East Germany. But that is another story...

The story I am going to tell you now is the reason I left the Army. I could have been commissioned to a Captain, but for the following reason I had to end my career. Unfortunately, I have two children with a life limiting condition who need a lot of care. This is their story...

I was thirty-five years old and had just taken over the post of Battery Sergeant Major, which is the top soldier in a sub unit in charge of about 100 men. Life was so good. My career was going really well and I had two healthy sons, who were ten and seven. I was at the local hospital, as my wife was giving birth to my daughter. My daughter Lucy was born early in the morning and I was thrilled as I held her in my arms, thinking to myself, I have two sons, and now the family is complete with the birth of my little girl.

My wife, though, kept saying, "I think there is something wrong with her."

I replied, "Don't be stupid, she's fine."

The doctor looked at her and said, "She *is* healthy."

But my wife knew something was wrong. I went home and later that night I got a phone call saying I needed to get back to the hospital, as they were concerned about some issues with Lucy.

When I arrived at the hospital, Lucy had been moved to the intensive care unit and was having a fit. She was lying there, kicking her tiny legs up and down. She had been fitting for two hours. I asked what was wrong, and they could only say they didn't know. I just thought it was some small problem that would be sorted out quickly, and wasn't overly concerned.

The doctor then said, "We need to move her to a specialist hospital twenty miles away, and we need to do it quickly."

It was at that moment it started to hit home that this was serious. She was moved to a high dependency unit and spent four days having tests. Lucy stopped fitting and started to improve, and she looked like any other new born baby. The doctors said she was going to be fine, and I started to think everything would be okay after all.

Then, on day five, the doctor came up to me and said, "I need to have a word with you in my office."

I entered the office, where two nurses sat waiting for me, and I knew what he had to tell me wasn't going to be good. He drew a large circle on a piece of paper and then shaded half of it in. He explained that they had taken scans of my daughter's brain and they had found damage. The shaded in area was the damaged part of Lucy's brain.

He said, "At this stage, we're not sure how it will effect her, but she will be either mentally or physically damaged." My heart sank, but I just thought, well, they said she *might* be mentally or physically ill. I thought she might not have problems and she could still come through all of this. I thought it over and just decided she would be okay. This is how I handle situations like this, by always looking at the positives and not the negatives.

Two weeks later, I had to go to another appointment at the hospital. They were doing a more detailed scan on Lucy. I was called into the same office.

The doctor said, "I'm sorry, but the damage is worse than we thought. Your daughter has sustained seventy-five percent damage to her brain, and she'll die at a young age. She will definitely be mentally and physically damaged."

I just went numb. Unless you've been in this situation, you can't understand the pain of being told that your child will die. I am a strong person, but that hurt like no other pain I had experienced before. I asked what had caused the damage, and was told there was no explanation; it was just one of those things and was probably due to her being starved of oxygen at some point during the birth.

I walked out of the hospital and sat in my car. I cried like a baby and didn't stop crying for three days. I had two options: crumble and look for sympathy, or crack on and get on with it. I decided on the latter.

This all happened when I had just started one of the most senior appointments in the Regiment, and I had to be at the top of my game. I decided to treat Lucy as a normal child, to give her all the love I could, and to do whatever I needed to in order to look after her. I didn't want my two other sons to be affected by any of this, either. I told my RSM that I wanted to be treated like any of the other Battery Sergeant Majors, and I didn't want any special treatment or sympathy. I told him I would still do my job well. He expressed his concern for me, and said he was there if I needed him.

I cracked on with my soldiering, and also with looking after Lucy. It was especially hard when it came to the time when she should be developing, doing things like crawling or walking, but of course, she could do none of these things. We had lots of hospital appointments and she was on all sorts of different medicines. I used to be up with her all night. I'd get two hours sleep and then go to work, and my wife would look after her during the day. She couldn't feed properly, so she had a tube put directly into her stomach, where the food was poured in to her. Soon, she was diagnosed as being blind. But she could hear, so she could be stimulated by sound. The care and support we got from the NHS was brilliant. We had a whole team of medical specialists, as well as carers to look after her from time to time, to give us a break.

I continued with my career, and was promoted to Warrant Officer Class One, and was then posted to the south of England. We decided to buy our own house so we could have a steady base for Lucy, as moving every two years wouldn't be good for her, due mostly to having to find a different specialist to look after her. The down side of this choice was that I had to work away, and was only home at weekends. We asked if we were safe to have another baby, as we had two healthy children, and there was no explanation for Lucy's brain damage.

We were told yes. It was safe.

Nine months later, our son James was born. As I held him in my arms, I remember saying, "he's okay," and I was so relieved. The doctors gave him a good check over and said he was fine. That night, I went home, and in the morning received a phone call from my wife saying I had better get to the hospital. It had happened again.

I couldn't believe it. I felt sick and was in total shock. I arrived at the hospital and went through the whole experience again. At one stage, I had to watch as they resuscitated James, as he had stopped breathing. Due to the fact we now had two children with the same illness, the hospital took skin samples from my children so they could send them for tests in London, to find out if they had some sort of genetic illness.

The test came back positive and my children were diagnosed with Pyruvate Dehydrogenase Deficiency. The disease is so rare that only twenty-four children world-wide had been diagnosed with it at that time. Basically, it's a deficiency of the gene that produces energy, and without that, your body can't function. We carried on as before, but now looking after two ill children. When James was about eight months old, I came home to find my wife completely worn out from looking after two ill children, as well as two healthy ones. I decided it was time to leave the army and spend more time at home looking after them.

I felt that being away eight months a year wasn't being a good dad. Time was limited with them as it was. The right thing to do was to give up my career and to spend as much time as possible with Lucy and James. By doing this, I could at least hold my head up high and say that I did everything possible for them whilst they were alive. Both children need twenty-four hour care. Lucy is blind, but James can see out of one eye. They will wear nappies until they die, they both get fed through a tube in their stomachs, and both are on a special diet. They can't walk or talk, and they will die at a young age.

This experience taught me so much about life. All I can say to people is, if you worry about silly things, such as the car having a scratch on it, or the carpet having a stain, then don't, because as long as you've got your heath, there's nothing to worry about. You never know what's around the corner, so make the most of things when they're going well. If dealt a hand like I was, then get on with it and make the most of the positives.

Lucy and James are so happy in their little world. They experience so many problems heath wise, and are in pain on many occasions, but they are smiling, happy children. Simple things, such as a strange noise or smell, will make them smile. They have a normal life, as far as it can be for them; they go to a special school, one of the happiest places I have known. The organisations that get involved with children like this are so special, such as the children's hospice, where they go and stay for two weeks a year. Lucy is now fifteen and James is twelve. They're so brave and strong, and have an amazing will to survive, so hopefully they'll prove the doctors wrong and live a long, happy life.

For those who have read this story, the next time you feel low, just remember there are children out there who were never given the opportunity to be in the position you are in. Please, make the most of what you have.

THE JOURNEY
BY MAUREEN HALEY MCDONALD

We were walking down the street one day, going from my house to his, when Ben suddenly stopped and said I'm thinking of joining the army. What? Why? I asked. He said he wanted to do more with his life and wanted to make something of himself, not be stuck in the same job in the same town for the rest of his life. I didn't try to talk him out of it because I knew him well enough to know that if he had mentioned it, he would do it come what may, I could see it in his eyes. From that moment I knew my life was about to change, and I was scared and worried. It would either be the end of us, or we would stay together and I would soon be moving away from my home and my family.

I had started going out with my boyfriend Ben when I was just 15 and he was 16 years old. I was still at school and he worked at the local butchers. I was quite shy, he was very outgoing. We had fun, we laughed a lot, and life was good. We enjoyed each other's company and spent a lot of time together.

Being the youngest of seven children, our house was always noisy and full of people. At this time there was only my sister Ann and myself still at home with Mum and Dad, but the others often visited with their families, so the noise continued. We lived on a council estate and went to a local school where we both had many friends, who were often at the house as well. I still had uncles serving in the Army, and when they were home on leave they would always visit with their families. Our house was a 'busy' house.

Ben went to the Army Careers office alone and called in to see me afterwards, to tell me he had to go back to do his test in a couple of days. He took his tests, and then the fitness tests, and finally found out he had been accepted into the British Army. He was given a date for joining up, which would be a couple of months away. My heart sank. Part of me hoped that he might change his mind and not go ahead with this crazy idea. I couldn't stop thinking about how different my life would be during the next few weeks, month, years.

On the day he left I knew it would be difficult, as he was about to start his basic training at Aldershot and we wouldn't see each other for some time. Christmas would fall within this period and we didn't know if he'd make it home for the holidays. It looked daunting to me.

In the early days, I got letters and the odd phone call to say how much he hated every minute of it and that he was definitely coming out after basic training. He really hated the 'crap' that they had to put up with and found it hard to take. He used to put letters for his mum inside my letters and ask me to take them to her, claiming that he was doing this to save on postage, but I was sure it was so that I would still go and visit his parents. His mum's letters contained the same information; I hate it here and I'm definitely coming out, I can't stand it, the only thing that keeps me going are the lads, they're a great bunch (mostly!). His mum told me to encourage him to stay in and not ask him to come home. She wanted him to stay in and make something of himself too, and she thought he just wanted to come home because he was missing me. Each time I visited with a letter she would say the same thing; "Now, you're not encouraging him to come out, are you?" My reply was always, "No, I'm not" and I didn't. It had to be his choice. I missed him terribly and really wanted him to come home but this wasn't about me, it was about Ben and his career choice. In my heart I knew he would do well and eventually enjoy a fulfilling career with the army. During this time I kept myself busy by going to the gym often, and I started to knit Ben a jumper for Christmas which I couldn't wait to see him in – I really hoped he would be home for Christmas day to receive it!

After a couple of months he began to sound happier, like he'd gotten used to it, and he was thrilled to be told that they would all be going home for Christmas. We talked about him staying in and he spoke of 47 Air Despatch Squadron, which he wanted to join. We set a date for our wedding and suddenly, I couldn't wait to join him and be a part of the exciting new life he had created for himself. I knew it was what Ben wanted, and I certainly didn't want to be without him. I wanted to experience forces life the way Ben had explained it to be. It sounded thrilling, and I was so relieved to know that Ben wanted me to be with him on this journey.

We were married on 28th April 1984. I was nineteen years old and he was twenty. He settled in at RAF Lyneham as a driver with 47 Air Despatch Squadron and undertook his training with them whilst we waited anxiously for a married quarter. Eventually, we were awarded one. I was still living at home with my parents during and when I got the phone call to tell me we had been allocated a married quarter, I was thrilled. That emotion was short lived, though, as I then had to tell my mum. I knew she would be heartbroken that her youngest child was about to leave home and move over a hundred miles away. She was very upset and it suddenly hit me that I wouldn't be seeing my family every day as I had been used to. What a mixture of emotions! I was extremely close to my family and really didn't want to leave them, but at the same time I knew it was time to move on with my life. The hardest part was seeing my mum upset and knowing I had caused her pain.

We didn't have a lot of things to take with us, but we had too much to fit in a car, so Ben asked his Sergeant if he could use one of the trucks to come and pick me up, along with the few belongings we had. (This would usually be a definite NO, as civilians were not allowed in army vehicles). After some persuasion the Sergeant said, "Oh, go on then, as long as you buy us a crate of beer!"

On a cold and wet November morning, my husband arrived at my parent's house, in an army truck, to take me to my new home. My mum had taken the day off work to wave me off, and all my family were there too, each one very upset. I cried as I hugged each one goodbye and my sister-in-law and I hung on to each other like we were never going to see each other again. I was still crying as Ben helped me into the truck. After saying goodbye to everyone, we were on our way, our new life ahead of us. Although I was really excited about the future, at that moment, I really didn't want to go.

We were about half way to our destination and the truck started to struggle. I asked what was wrong, but Ben didn't know. After making several stops to see if he could sort out the problem, it was time to call his Sergeant and explain that we had broken down. He knew he was in for an ear bashing. He was told to drive to the nearest Army base and they would arrange for another truck to meet him there tomorrow. Tomorrow! So what do we do now? We drove to the Army base as Ben had been instructed and felt such fools as the truck spluttered over to the guard room. Ben met with a Sergeant there and I waited in the truck. He didn't say much when he got back, but I could see he was in big trouble for having me with him. He was told that one of the duty drivers would take us into town to help us to find a hotel for the night, and tomorrow they would swap the trucks over. The duty driver took us to the nearest hotel but as it was now about ten pm, they didn't answer the door. We drove around looking for other hotels and if the landlords did answer, they had no rooms. We were like Mary and Joseph, nowhere to stay or rest for the night. I was beside myself and could see that Ben was really worried about what the outcome might be. We managed to find a room after about forty-five minutes of knocking on doors and we were settled for the night. The duty driver was a great lad and arranged to come back at seven-thirty in the morning to pick Ben up, so that he could swap over the trucks. The next morning Ben went off to camp and I stayed in the room for most of the day. The landlady knocked at the door to ask what I would like to eat, and she ended up staying with me for a couple of hours as I told her what had happened, and cried some more. A lovely, kind lady.

Later on in the afternoon, Ben arrived with a new truck after transferring our belongings into the back. I'm sure, as an inexperienced soldier, he must have been very worried about what might happen when we got to Lyneham. We paid for our room and left. Once again we were on our way – not a very good start to our new life. (Ben did get in trouble but nothing serious, his sergeant handled it very well.)

We arrived at RAF Lyneham to pick up the keys and someone came with us to show us around and do the usual checks. We loved the house in a quiet caul-de-sac and a little play area at the back of our garden. Our neighbours were all RAF and we were the only Army. As the first few days went by we unpacked our belongings and settled in. We literally had an iron, an ironing board, a portable black and white TV and an old stereo record player, as well as kitchen utensils and linen. The first thing we brought was a washing machine, and for the first time ever I had to do the washing. I was missing home a lot and I couldn't get used to the silence of the house. I always had music on to keep me company during the long days alone. I cried every day for the first month, and Ben used to come home from work at lunchtime just to make sure I was still there, as he thought I would go back home. I didn't.

Soon, some of the neighbours popped in to introduce themselves and stayed for coffee, and one evening Ben told me that one of the other lads from the squadron had recently got married and had been allocated a married quarter at the end of the week, so his wife would be joining him from Northern Ireland. I was looking forward to meeting her and hoping that we would get on and become friends. I really needed a friend right now.

After a couple of weeks of being in our new home, Ben had to go away on an exercise. I remember thinking, "it's a good job I can drive." The shops weren't close enough to do your weekly shopping if you had to walk. So off I went to do some shopping. I called in at the petrol station on the way to fill up with fuel and saw a notice in the window for a Forecourt Cashier. Without even thinking, I applied for it and got the job! I started work whilst Ben was away and when he rang I told him I had a job. He laughed and said, "So much for you not working." He knew I would find a job, I'm not one for staying at home and getting bored. Ben and I had talked about me not having to work, but deep down I knew I would. The thought of never having to work sounded good, but in reality it would drive me insane being at home alone every day.

I met my new friend Amy, from Northern Ireland, and she was lovely. We also met another army wife called Hannah, and she was great fun. Although we eventually met many other army wives, the three of us stuck together and we had some great times. We kept each other going when the lads were away, and we became very good friends.

Having a job helped me to settle into RAF Lyneham and forces life. I felt suddenly 'grown up'. We were making a new life together, and I was starting to get used to it. Although we were enjoying it, it was also extremely hard, especially when Ben had to go away (which seemed to be often). I loved army life but at the same time I hated it. I still missed my family a lot and wanted to be closer to home. Life seemed to be an emotional roller coaster at times.

As time went on, visitors from home started to arrive; my parents, Ben's parents, my brothers and sisters with their families, and of course our friends. They would all stay for a few days and we took great pleasure in showing them around. On the visits when my mum came alone for a week at a time, I would take her out and about in the car and she was amazed how I could find my way around everywhere (you have no choice when your husband's away all the time, you just get on with it!). I could tell that she was very proud of me and although she missed me being at home, she was also confident that I was safe and happy. Her youngest child was all grown up.

Our visits back home were quite rare, as Ben didn't seem to get much time off. Even when he was on leave there seemed to be something going on that meant we had to stay local. When we did go home everyone was really excited to see us and there was always a lot of invitations. I was extremely close to my family and on one visit my two nieces, aged fourteen and fifteen, were feeling really fed up, as they were on holiday from school. I suggested they come back with us for the week. Well, you would have thought they had won the lottery! They were up and bags packed in no time, and I said to Ben, "it looks like they're coming with us!" He didn't mind. Both of us would be working, but at least it was a change of scenery for the girls. Halfway through the week we took them to the NAAFI disco on camp. The single lads were all around them and Marie and Jayne were loving it! Ben wasn't impressed and I didn't realise how difficult it was trying to keep two teenage girls away from burly soldiers! We spent the night checking where they were and who with! We managed to get them back to our home safely, but they just giggled and asked when they would be allowed to go again. "Never!" was my sharp reply. I found it a huge responsibility looking after two teenage girls when I was only twenty years old myself! We got on really well and I hated saying goodbye to them as they got on the coach back to Swindon. We were all really upset and they started to shout, "Please don't make us go Mum, I promise I'll behave if you let me stay." Everyone was looking at them and I was very embarrassed. They continued the joke as the coach pulled away and they were banging on the window! Little monkeys! I drove home in tears, missing them so much, and knowing that I was going back to an empty house.

Four years went by and we were blessed with a beautiful little girl called Corrine. She was a delight, and we were very settled in our little home, but we began to feel that Army life wouldn't be good for children. We spoke about what we wanted for the future, and we both agreed that we didn't want our children to have to go to many different schools, and we definitely wouldn't be sending them to boarding school. Anyway, we made the decision, and because of this, Ben decided he wouldn't be staying in the army for many more years, because he wanted to leave before Corrine started school.

With that in mind, he came home from work one day and said, "How do you feel about a posting to Germany?" I was shocked. We had been in Lyneham for four years; we loved it, we loved our home, our friends, Ben loved his job – so why? Ben had decided that as he was only planning to stay in for a few more years, he might as well experience more of what the army had to offer – which meant an overseas posting. He spoke to his RSM and explained his reasons for wanting the new posting. We spoke about it, but I felt it had to be Ben's decision in the end. Soon after, Ben was told he would be joining 2 Armoured Field Ambulance in Osnabruck, Germany. As we packed up our belongings, we were both apprehensive about the move, and didn't know if we had made the right decision.

It was three weeks before Corrine's first birthday, and we had just arrived in Germany. Although we had both been on holidays abroad before, neither of us had been to Germany, so we didn't know what to expect. It was late afternoon when we went to the camp to collect the keys to our married quarter, only to be told that our belongings wouldn't arrive until tomorrow. Great! The only thing we had with us were Corrine's baby items! We got to our quarter, an upstairs maisonette (that wouldn't be easy with a baby and a pram to carry up and down the stairs!) We weren't in the best of moods when we settled down for the night.

Corrine was in an army issue cot, but we had brought her sheets and blankets with us, luckily. Ben and I slept on the floor with a blanket. I say slept, but we didn't sleep at all. The next morning Ben went off to camp to start his new post. Our belongings arrived later that day and boy, was I relieved. When Ben arrived home from work, he told me he was going away on exercise for a few weeks. He had been gone for a week when Corrine started to become poorly. I took her to the medical centre on camp, and it turned out she had mumps. Two days later was Corrine's first birthday. She had received many presents from family and friends and we had brought her a paddling pool. When she woke up that morning I fetched her from her cot and she beamed a beautiful little smile even though she was really poorly. I took her into the lounge where I had blown up her paddling pool and put the presents inside for her to open. She wasn't her normal self, but still managed a smile or a little chuckle whilst we opened the presents. Later on that morning when Corrine was back in her cot, I sat and cried. What a birthday. Not that she understood any different, but her daddy should be there. Home seemed a long way away, and I felt very, very lonely. I couldn't wait for Ben to get back.

We tried to like Germany, we really did. I took Corrine to a mothers and toddlers group, which she loved, and I joined a netball team. We made some lovely friends but I was really home sick and Ben didn't get the same buzz from his job that he had with 47AD. After a year, we decided that Germany wasn't for us. Ben had decided it was time to leave the Army, and as I had just found out that I was pregnant, we longed for a normal life – whatever that was. Ben spoke to his RSM and said that he wanted to get out of the army, but his RSM really didn't want him to leave and offered him a posting back to the UK. We decided that this was a good idea, as it would give us the chance to look around for a house of our own to purchase once Ben got out. We agreed, and were lucky enough to get a posting to RAF Brize Norton in Oxfordshire. I was thrilled, we both were, and we knew it was the right thing to do.

I absolutely loved our new home. It was an end house in a quiet cul-de-sac. We soon got to know the neighbours and they were great. Ben loved his job and happiness resumed! We were closer to home and had a steady flow of visitors again. It was always good to see everyone. We always stayed at our own home for Christmas, and tried to get home for New Year when Ben wasn't on duty.

Soon after settling into our new home, our little boy Jordan was born. He made our family complete and we adored him. Then, when Jordan was just six weeks old, I had a visit from an officer and a sergeant. I knew something was wrong as soon as I saw them. They told me that Ben had had an accident at work and was in hospital, twenty-six miles away. He had been crushed between two vehicles and had broken his coccyx (bottom of his spine). I felt numb. I wasn't sure what to do or say. I was obviously in shock. I had a two year old daughter and a six week old baby to look after, as well as a husband who was in hospital. The officer assured me that I would have all the support I needed from the squadron, and I did. Some of Ben's friends offered to babysit whilst I visited him in hospital, but that wasn't easy, as they hardly knew the children, and Jordan was so young. I couldn't expect a young, single lad to look after a six week old baby and a young child— Lord knows I wasn't finding it easy myself, but they had no experience whatsoever! That first night one of Ben's very good friends Paul and his wife Claire looked after the children whilst I made my way to visit Ben at RAF Wroughton Hospital. Ben was in a lot of pain and still undergoing tests on that first visit. I felt really sorry for him, but also felt angry with him for putting me in this situation. It was an emotional time.

Ben told me not to worry about him, to concentrate on the children as they needed me more – but they all needed me. I felt like I was spinning plates, trying to look after them all. The next day, after about two hours sleep, I phoned my sister Tracey in tears. Tracey got the next coach to Swindon and I picked her up from there. She came to help me with the children so that I could visit Ben. Through the night, Jordan woke for a feed every hour and would only take 1oz of milk at a time, and Tracey stayed up to feed him so that I could get some sleep. She was a star, and to this day I don't know how I would have got through that situation without her. The army were fantastic, but I just couldn't leave my children with anyone else, as I'm sure most other new mums would understand. Tracey stayed with me until Ben was released from hospital.

As the children grew older, Ben wanted more than ever to leave the army, and we spoke about what he might do when he left. We'd had a good life so far, but it wasn't what we wanted for our young family. When Corrine was three and Jordan was just a year old, Ben spoke to Staffordshire Fire & Rescue Service to enquire about becoming a Fire Fighter. They said that they only advertise twice a year, usually in the local newspaper. Ben explained that he didn't live in that area, so he wouldn't see the job advert and asked if they would send him an application form when they were next recruiting and they agreed. Some months later, as I picked up the post, I saw a letter addressed to Ben with Staffordshire Fire & Rescue Service printed on it. I knew immediately what it was and I so wanted to hide it and forget about it, but I couldn't. In some ways I wanted life to stand still. We were a happy family, life was good now, and I didn't want that to change. But we had to do what we thought was right for the children as well as ourselves. They deserved to know their family back home and to spend more time with them. This was the way forward, and Ben had had enough of the army. It's strange really, all my life-changing experiences have depended on Ben's decisions, and this was no exception! As I handed the envelope to Ben that evening, I knew the next chapter was about to begin.

For all the heartache and loneliness, the difficult decisions, moving houses, not knowing anyone but making new friends, this has been a journey that has made me who I am today. I'm a strong individual who is able to cope in a crisis, and can make informed decisions at the drop of a hat because, at times, I had to. Would I do it all over again? You bet I would!

MY AFGHANISTAN STORY
BY JOHNO

I am shaking, wet through with sweat. I can taste the sand in my mouth. I can smell the burnt flesh and dust. I can feel the searing heat on my face. I can hear the screams and the noise of the helicopter.

I wake. It takes me a second to realise where I am. It's one in the morning, I am at home in my house in a quiet village in Nottinghamshire, and I've been locked in a nightmare.

It's probably better if I start from the beginning, or the beginning of this story, anyway. My name is Johnathan Lee, Johno to my mates, or Lee, as the army knows me. I was an acting Lance Corporal and this was my first tour of Afghanistan. It was my second war zone, having served in Iraq, and it was my third active tour.

It was the 6th of November 2007, 4:30a.m. Afghanistan time. I'd woken up and the first thing I did was go and get a shave and wash. That was a luxury in Afghanistan, but I was in a forward operating base that had the Norwegian Army and the American Special Forces, so this was quite a lavish camp, compared to others. Well, it had running water, toilets, a shop, and a cookhouse. My fellow colleagues at different forward operating bases didn't have such luxuries. Their luxuries included a hole to piss in and sand bags to keep them from getting shot.

I looked at my reflection in the mirror.

I was 6'3", lean and muscled, with a shaved head. At twenty-five I looked very young, but made up for it with my experience. After having a wash, I went to the cookhouse and had a big breakfast. The Americans know how to look after their men, so I had a full English with cereal. You eat well, while you can. You never know when your next hot meal will be. I returned to my accommodation, an army tent shared with twelve other squaddies. They were large, sandy coloured tents that got very hot in the day and very cold at night. We also had the luxury of cot beds to sleep on, rather than the ground.

This particular morning, I was due out on an early-morning patrol, so I went through my usual solitary routine. First, I would completely remove any identification. This meant ID cards, drivers license, and letters from home, anything that could say who I was in case I was captured. The reason for this was simple. If I was captured, or my dead body got taken by the enemy, I wanted to make sure they would have no way of getting to my family back home. A driver's licence, or letters with their address, would make it easier for them to do so.

Second, I made sure we had the kit to fight for our lives if it came down to it. My machine-gun, my rifle, and my pistol were completely stripped down, oiled, cleaned, and ready to use. Also, I checked the stock of the vehicle. There were 10,000 rounds, plus a rocket launcher and two boxes of grenades, as well as signals equipment, a first-aid kit, a mine-marking kit, water, and emergency rations.

Then it came down to prepping myself. Every soldier has a routine. Mine started from the bottom and worked up. I would tie my boots and tape the laces so they wouldn't come undone. I'd fasten up my jacket and in the left jacket pocket I would put a tourniquet, and mark the pocket with a Red Cross and an O+ as my blood-group. This was just in case anyone needed to stop me from bleeding. If you got injured, you couldn't guarantee it would be British medical team treating you, so any extra information was a good idea. In the opposite pocket went my camera. Afghanistan may be a war zone, but it is also a beautiful country and when possible I would take a few snaps. Next up came my body armour. This went on top, and then my chest rigging went over it. The rigging contained six magazines for my rifle, two magazines for my pistol, and one bandolier for my machine gun. It also contained morphine, a second tourniquet, first field dressings and a mine kit. In my grab bag I had a night sight, an extra 4000 rounds, plus some more grenades, water, and beef jerky. Patrols could last a long time. Next up, my helmet, again with my blood group on it, and last of all my 'smag'. That was a sandy coloured scarf I used to wrap around my face to keep the sand out. Last, my ballistic sunglasses went on. During the night I had see-through white lenses, but during the day I would fix red lenses to them.

This process took me about thirty minutes. We used to do this for every patrol to make sure we had the right kit for every occurrence, which could include:

- Straight forward enemy attack

- IED (improvised explosive device or mine)

- Land mines

- Ambush

- Suicide bomber (child or woman)

- Suicide donkey (a donkey stuffed with explosives. They were very inventive)

And obviously, the worst case scenario, which was making sure you had enough kit to deny the vehicle from the enemy, and ultimately, to deny them yourself, if it came down to it.

Our job overview, in Afghanistan, was to train and mentor the Afghan National Army. So prior to departure we had the day's brief by our platoon commander.

Our mission that day was for my team of nine, call sign OMLT 4 ALPHA, (described as a multiple), to meet up with the Afghan National Army at their camp, which was about a five-minute drive away. We would then take them on a patrol through Gereshk, which was another thirty minutes away. There, we would collect two more British units. We would then carry on to a forward operating base approximately two hours away through the desert and resupply them. Once this was completed, we would return back to camp.

One other piece of news we received was that there was a suspected suicide bomber in the area.

My job as Signaller/Top Cover was to be capable of physically protecting an individual from enemy fire, as well as spotting for mines, IEDs, suicide bombers, or any other possible threat to the unit and convoy. To achieve this, I would stand up on a vehicle moving at 60mph, which I can only describe as popping my torso out of the sunroof, whilst trying to spot the enemy or anything suspicious. At the same time, I had to avoid being shot or blown up myself.

The day started badly, with me having a row with my platoon commander an hour before we went out on patrol. The vehicles we were supposed to be using had been switched at the last minute, and we were using a Land Rover variant I felt wasn't compatible with the mission that morning. Due to our row, the commander switched me from lead vehicle to second vehicle, saying, "You can stop moaning, you'll be safe in the second vehicle." Normally, the front and rear vehicles get the worst of any contacts, and as we were a three-vehicle convoy, his theory seemed sound.

The sun had just started to rise and the rumble of the engines of our vehicles filled the camp. One last check of our kit, and we were ready to go.

We left camp and made our way to meet the Afghan National Army and, after a five minute journey, we arrived without any nasty surprises. The Afghans used an old Russian compound, which the Russians had probably acquired from the locals during their ill-fated attempt at controlling Afghanistan. The compound was surrounded by walls that looked about 100 years old. They were ten feet tall and made of mud. What made the Afghans feel a lot safer was the fact that it was surrounded by a Russian minefield. The compound wall had holes from old battles, and had an old rusty iron gate at its entry. The gate was secured by two Afghan soldiers, who were fast asleep. Not surprisingly, the rest of the Afghan National Army were also still asleep, but after a few chosen words from the platoon commander, they started to get a move on.

After waiting around for about half an hour, only four of the Afghan National Army decided to come on patrol, in a single white pickup vehicle. So much for commitment. We eventually moved off towards central Gereshk. Gereshk is located on the important transport route known as Highway 1, which was built during the time of the Soviet war in Afghanistan. This route links Farah Province in the west to Kandahar Province in the east. At this time in the morning, there was very little traffic on the road. The only vehicles we saw were large HGV style vehicles with massive amounts of cargo. Although they appeared strapped down, it seemed like only good luck and gravity kept them there. Some of the vehicles had missing doors and bonnets, and had battle scars with bullet marks and smashed windows. Probably from run-ins with local militias.

We arrived at Gereshk and entered the compound in the centre of town that held the British forces and the Afghan National Army. It was an old police compound that had been reinforced with sand bags, and military structures made out of reinforced concrete. Gereshk had just started to wake up. Cockerels were just getting going, adding to the noise from people setting up market stalls and the odd car on the road. The locals that were awake gave us suspicious looks as we entered. They certainly kept us on our toes. We quickly joined up with the other unit, call sign OMLT4 BRAVO. They were using two, larger wheeled armoured vehicles. The convoy was ready and we set off. In the front vehicle was the commander, the driver, a photographer we picked up from Gereshk, who was working for the British Army, and an interpreter we had also picked up in Gereshk. And of course, my replacement, the guy the commander opted for instead of me. In the second vehicle with me were two TA members, one of whom was a driver, the other a 2ndLieutenant. In the third vehicle there was colour sergeant from the guards, a driver and a top cover. Behind them were the two vehicles that had just joined us, and bringing up the rear was the Afghan National Army in a pickup truck, with an Afghan commander and two guys in the back, one with an RPG on, one with a machine gun. We then set off to the operating base, call sign STAMFORD.

By the time we set off, the market was getting pretty busy. It felt hostile and unwelcoming with the amount of people around. I had to use my voice and my weapon to intimidate people, to keep them away from our convoy just in case they had other ideas. Anybody coming within fifteen metres of the vehicle would get a verbal warning, followed immediately with a warning shot. If they had continued to approach I would have opened fire. No messing about. Suicide bombers don't value life. Luckily this morning everybody stayed out of our way. A few groups of males covered head to toe in head scarfs and Arabic style clothing eyed up our convoy, but we knew who they were. We called them "Dickers". They were used by the Taliban and foreign fighters to get as much information on us as they could. Thankfully our time in central Gereshk passed without incident. So we moved onwards, to forward operating base STAMFORD.

The route was long and bleak and the temperature was rising by the minute.

The dessert was rocky and stony, with deep crevices all around. There were no trees or grass anywhere. Everything was just dirty and dusty. Also, there were no people or cars. Not even a goat, and there were plenty goats in Afghanistan. As we pushed on, my machine gun rocked, bumped, and jarred with every pot hole we hit. My arms burned with the heat of my weapon and the sharp screws on the vehicle cut into my arms.

It was difficult to concentrate, but you had to. The safety of the convoy depended on me and the other guy in the vehicle behind. Then something got my attention. There was a fire about two miles away, and then I saw a second one. I knew this was an old form of communication used by the Taliban. My heart started to pump. I scanned the horizon and shouted down to the driver and 2nd lieutenant. I told them I had a funny feeling something wasn't right. The 2nd lieutenant looked at me and told me everything was fine and not to worry. He told me it'd been a long morning and to get some water. So I grabbed a bottle of water, had a quick sip, repositioned my legs and stood up. I quickly had a look on the horizon and saw the lead vehicle in front.

And then...I remember feeling funny, not really knowing where I was, and all of a sudden there was a massive bang to my helmet. I went unconscious.

When I came to, I was confused. There was dust everywhere. All I could smell was burning skin and sand. I fell unconscious again. I came around and I could hear somebody screaming. It was the driver, screaming my name. The sand and dust were everywhere. Then I started to focus. I looked for the other vehicles. The lead vehicle was about fifty metres in front and stationary. I looked back at my vehicle. It was on its side, facing the opposite direction. The wheel arch was completely blown away, the wheel was gone, and the metal had been completely bent out of all recognition. I screamed, "What the fuck has happened?" and there was complete silence. Finally, I got a reply.

"Johno, we've been blown up. Are you okay?"

I started to panic, and shouted that I couldn't feel my legs. I didn't know where I was, and black dust was everywhere. I couldn't see anything, my senses were gone.

I shouted, "I think I've lost my legs, I can't feel my legs." I started to panic.

"Johno, keep still, I'll get you."

I think I dropped back unconscious again, because the next thing I heard was voices from behind me. I turned my head to see the driver on what I thought was the top of the vehicle, but was actually the side. He was screaming, "Johno, I can see you, are you all right?"

The sand was starting to settle and there was a soft blanket of fine dust in the air. I look down at my legs and saw they were there. I said, "My legs are here." I cannot express the relief I felt, just seeing two legs where they were supposed to be.

"Johno, I need you to check your testicles, mate."

Thankfully, they were there too. We started to laugh.

Although I was still in a daze, things started to clear and I realised what happened. We had hit some sort of explosive device. My right foot had been positioned on top of the wheel arch, the wheel arch that activated the explosive device, and was blown to bits. I guessed that the vehicle had flipped over and thrown me into the air. The vehicle landed facing the opposite direction, and then fell on its side. I had gone about ten metres the other way, and landed head-first in the desert. The explosion could have ignited all the ammunition and grenades we were carrying, sending shrapnel everywhere, but thankfully nothing exploded and nothing went off.

My kit had been ripped apart and my weapon was nowhere

to be seen. I quickly told the two people in my vehicle my weapon was missing. The driver told me he could see it about nine metres away from the vehicle, but the barrel was bent. I remember thinking I had no way to defend myself if we came under attack. I was completely defenceless and of no use to my team if we came under fire.

I tried to stand up. Big, big mistake. As I put weight on my legs I felt the most pain I've ever felt in my entire life. The scream that came out of me surprised even me. I looked at my right leg. My knee was pointing one way, and my foot the other. I guessed I had broken it, but I couldn't see as I couldn't move my combat trousers. My left leg didn't seem as bad, but there was definitely a problem with the ankle. But there was one thing I could confirm. I was in pain. Lots of pain. I took a deep breath, turned around, and said, "I've broken my legs."

I didn't want to panic them too much, as I knew it wouldn't help them or myself, and we weren't sure if there were any more explosive devices in the area. Now some choices had to be made.

•Choice one: Get a team from one of the other vehicles to come rescue us all.

•Choice two: Try and get ourselves out.

While I waited for the decision, I decided I was going to try and get myself back to what I thought was the safest place in the world, my vehicle. I started to drag my legs and myself backwards. I was in complete agony, but I needed to succeed. With my hands and my nails digging in the ground, I gave everything I had. Two more metres. I was nearly there. I took another deep breath...

"Johno, STOP."

I looked back, and the driver was screaming at me to stop. He had seen a landmine about a metre away from my head.

It was at that point that I realised I was probably going to die in the desert, that morning. The 2nd lieutenant in the vehicle asked me if I wanted him to send someone to retrieve me, as one of the other vehicles had a mine detector. I declined and told him to get the professionals in. Nobody should risk themselves to get me. I wasn't being brave; I just couldn't have lived with myself if somebody had died trying to retrieve me. At the time, I didn't fully realise what my injuries were, but I was pretty sure I was laying in a minefield.

So now the wait began. The commander called up an EOD (Explosive Ordnance Disposal) team. This was a helicopter unit that carried a medic and could also rescue my unit from the mine field. Time passed and with every minute it grew hotter. I needed a drink, and the only available water was in the upturned vehicle. After a brief discussion the driver threw me a bottle. The discussion went something like this—

"I'm thirsty. I need a drink."

"Want me to throw you a bottle?"

"Yes."

"You know if you drop it, it could set off a land mine and kill us all."

"I'd better not drop it then."

The EOD team took longer than expected, as there had been a suicide bomber in Gereshk that had blown himself up near the market. The one we had passed earlier. The one that had felt threatening. Turns out, it was.

This didn't help me, as the pain started to became too much. I retrieved a morphine syringe from my webbing and placed it on my leg. I pressed the red button and injected it into my system. This is where the fun began. Within a few seconds I felt the morphine whizzing through my body. The pain was still there, I was in agony, but it was dulled by the drug. I went delirious. It was like I had been out drinking all night and carried on drinking the next day. Time passed very slowly. I was lapsing in and out of consciousness for around forty minutes before I realised something wasn't right. I shouldn't be going in and out of consciousness, even on morphine. I started to go through the medical training I'd been given in the army.

I had gone unconscious when the explosion happened, that made sense, but going in and out of consciousness with a broken leg meant something wasn't right. I quickly started touching parts of my body with my hands, checking to see if there was blood. I checked all the parts I could reach. I even loosened my body armour and helmet to make sure I didn't miss anything.

My body was fine. Now it was time for the legs. I carefully moved them so I could touch the right side of my right leg. It was covered in blood. The sand underneath had soaked it up, which was why I couldn't see it until I moved my leg. Fuck, I was bleeding to death.

I took a deep breath, fumbled around in my pocket and grabbed my digital camera. I switched it to video, turned it on, and with tears in my eyes I said my final goodbyes to my family. I told them I loved them and I would see them soon. Then I heard shouting from the driver. He was shouting to get my attention, as I wasn't speaking to him and he was starting to panic. He had also realised something wasn't right.

He tried to speak to me about everything from what football team I support to what I wanted to do when I left the army, but I was too tired. I couldn't speak, I just wanted to go to sleep. I told him I would see him soon, and he asked me what I meant. I told him I didn't feel right, and something was wrong. At this point I told him there was a lot of blood coming from my leg. He told me to hold on.

Then I heard it. It was the helicopter. An Apache. An angel come to save me. Then a second, larger helicopter landed. This was the EOD team with the medic. The driver shouted to me.

"Johno, it isn't going to be long, hold on."

"I don't think I can. I'm not feeling too good." I then closed my eyes and very quietly said, "I'm ready to go. If you're going to take me it's now or never." I took a deep breath and counted down.

10.

9. I was at peace and not scared.

8. When you know you are dying, there is no need to be afraid. I was completely at ease.

7. At this point, for some strange reason, a song got into my head. It was Men of Harlech, a song from the movie Zulu, which I remembered watching with my dad when I was five.

6.

5.

4.

3.

2.
1. That was it. I took a last deep breath.

Then I heard rumbling behind me. It was one of the EOD team. He had managed to mine detect up to my vehicle. He shouted, "Hold on, I'll be there in a minute. I'm just helping your mates and I'll be back to get you."

Now survival kicked in. I knew I had to hold on, so I grabbed a bandage from my pocket and managed to wrap it around my ankle, hoping it would stabilise my leg. I knew when they came to move me, the quicker they could do it, the safer for us all.

Then I heard a voice from in front of me.

The person stood about six feet tall. He carried a mine detector. His first words could have been chosen better. He looked at me, grabbed his radio and said, "If we don't move this lad now, he's going to die. Get a medical up here, now."

I looked at him and said, "Thanks mate, I appreciate that." (A little bit of soldier sense of humour.)

"I just need to clear the area up to you, then I can get a medic to you."

I explained the drag marks right next to him were made by me, when I had crawled to my position, and I had also cleared the area around my chest. He asked me again what I had done, just to confirm he wasn't hearing things. He then looked at me and said confidently, "I'm going to get you out here." He stepped across to me and grabbed my hand. I pointed to my pocket and asked him to get the camera to my family. Then I went unconscious. The next time I woke, there were eight guys around me and a medic pumping me with some sort of milky liquid into my hand. They carried me to the helicopter and I thought I had passed out again. I didn't regain consciousness until I woke up in camp Bastian.

Well, that's what I thought. In reality, I was actually quite awake. I was told that I was screaming abuse at the people helping me onto the helicopter because my leg was moving and I was in absolute agony. I had broken the tibia and fibula of my right leg. Also, there was a hole on the underside of my foot, the size of the heel of my boots, and I had dislocated my knee. My left foot also had a break, but nowhere near as bad.

Finally, I had sustained shrapnel to my abdomen, upper torso, my arms and legs, and a piece of shrapnel to my chin had left an inch cut to my face. The only reason I managed to save my eyes were my ballistic sunglasses.

They got me onto the helicopter, and my heart stopped. They managed to revive me and got me to Camp Bastian, the main camp for British forces in Helmand province, Afghanistan. So now, while I have chance, I would like to apologise to the guys who saved me, and hope they understood. Sorry guys.

By the time we got to camp Bastian, I was awake. I remember being taken into the operating theatre, and the doctor coming over to me. I looked at him and told him that if they took my leg, I would hunt him down and kill him. It was really strange. Less than thirty minutes previously I was ready to die, but now I had been given a chance, and I was absolutely petrified I was going to lose my leg. After the operation, the first thing I did was ask if they had taken my leg. They told me that the doctor had to come and speak to me, and they couldn't answer my questions.

My heart sank. I thought, *fucking hell, I've lost my leg*. I tried to look, but couldn't see past my waist, as it was covered in a blanket. But I couldn't feel my legs at all. The doctor came and spoke to me. He said they had spared my leg, stabilised me and given me blood, but didn't think my leg was saveable. They had given me the best possible chance they could, and now they would send me back to the UK to see what they could do.

They also told me some gutting news

There had been a second explosion after I'd left, and one of my mates had received shrapnel to his face. He was okay and in the hospital and wanted to see me. Over the next few hours people from my regiment came to visit. Every time I fell under a morphine induced sleep, I would wake to find another member of my regiment visiting me. From my commanding officer to our Clerk and a Sgt called Lee, whom I'd beaten at poker a few days before, they all took time to visit. We were a very close regiment and every time we had down time we would arrange something to do together, from watching rugby to having a friendly game of poker. Sadly, Sgt Lee would lose his life three weeks later, in a mine blast.

Many more people came to see me, but sadly I only remember a few, as I was drugged up to the eyeballs.

I'm not sure how long I was there, but I wasn't there for long. Believing me to be stable, the decision was made to move me from Camp Bastian to the camp in Kandahar, and from there to fly directly to Birmingham International airport, then transfer to Selly Oak hospital in Birmingham.

However, I wasn't as stable as they thought. Just before the plane took off, my heart stopped and they had to get me off the plane. I was looked after by a Norwegian medical team, who joked about giving me Norwegian blood. It was all they had. Six hours later, I was stable and they loaded me onto a plane.

I began my journey back home.

STANDING BY
BY LISA WELLS

Some people know the very second their lives change. Some suffer life changing injuries, others make momentous personal decisions. For me, it was only looking back that I realised there was that moment, a day that changed everything!

My life was ticking along nicely, nothing exciting. I was a Sergeant in the RAF and had spent the last twenty-two years juggling being a single mother of two children with a full time military career. To be honest, life was just settling down. My two children were now older, with my daughter now twenty-two, with a three year old daughter of her own and another on the way. My son was seventeen, and looking ahead at his own future. I had my quiet future planned, just me and my dogs. Bliss.

I had been at RAF Wyton Cambridgeshire for less than a year when Corporal Justin Wells was posted in from Germany at the beginning of 2012. As my subordinate (yes, I was his boss) in a very small section, we got to know each other quite quickly. We would chat over coffee and I knew he had come back to the UK to assist his ageing parent. He lived with his partner, her two sons, and his own son, whom he had been looking after for some years. He seemed to have a stable home life. He was good at his job (even if he was ARMY), he involved himself in the office, joined in with the banter and accepted the verbal abuse regularly hurled at him (which was only fair, as he was the only Army member in an RAF office), joined in all the sport and activities, and was always immaculately turned out. In fact, he was Mr Military. He lived for the Army. To him it was the best thing since sliced bread, the only service to be in.

By mid 2012 I was comfortable enough with Justin to ask him to look in on my son from time to time while I carried out security duties at the London Olympics. On my return from the

Olympics at the end of August, everything seemed normal and I settled back into work.

A few weeks later, on a Sunday afternoon, I had a knock on the door. It was Justin...unusual, but I invited him in for a coffee. He was visibly upset, and it transpired that his partner at the time had asked him and his son to leave the house. His son was fifteen at the time, and in his final years of schooling. For the sake of his son, he saw no other option than to ask his ex-wife to look after him, so he could stay in his school and finish his education. I think that giving up his son was more upsetting for him than the breakdown of his relationship. But he did what all good military men do and soldiered on.

We chatted regularly over the next few weeks, becoming closer, but only as friends. I never thought of him as anything else, as I was his boss, and he had just had a bad break up from a relationship. I was worried about him but not greatly. He was still the jovial Army bloke in the office, still first in the morning and working hard, training hard, doing whatever was asked of him. What a shock, then, when he came in one morning clearly still drunk from the night before. Knowing he had lived in Germany for the last eighteen years and how much of the culture involves drinking, I knew he must have had a considerable amount to still be feeling the effects the next morning. Within minutes of arriving he pulled me to one side for a quiet word, and broke down immediately. It was obvious to me that this was beyond the normal mini crisis we see so often with junior members. Here was a mature, nearing middle-aged man, who was used to the trial and tribulations of life. I felt it was beyond my ability to deal with, that he needed professional help, and the best thing I could do was take him to the medical centre. They would be able to help him through this little blip, I was sure.

From seeing the practice manager (a friend) to the emergency doctor's appointment they quickly established he needed a specialist mental health assessment, the nearest of which was fifty miles away at RAF Marham. The whole time Justin looked terrified, was arguing at every turn, refusing to accept what they were saying, not wanting to go down the path he saw before him. But he knew me, and whether it was because I was his immediate superior and he was one for always taking orders, or we had just become good friends, he seemed to calm down a little and follow my instructions. I got the feeling he trusted me. Rather than put him in a car with a stranger to take him to RAF Marham, I offered to drive him myself. I needed to take care of my friend, and something told me I needed to be with him. Maybe these were the first signs that I had feelings for him, however, if they were, I completely ignored them. After all, it had been a long time since I had trusted anyone, and I had always been a sucker for a hard luck story.

The drive to RAF Marham wasn't bad. We laughed along the way, after all that's what we military people do in a crisis, but as we got closer his mood changed and he became quiet and withdrawn. Throughout the day I had been assuming that he was in crisis, brought on by the breakdown of his relationship and the difficult situation with his son.

Apart from his doctor's appointment back at RAF Wyton, I had been with him the whole time and I felt he needed me now, so I stayed with him while people came and went and asked this and that. I saw him dodge many questions, panic at some, and break down at others, all the time looking at me for reassurance like a child wanting you to make it all better. But I felt helpless. These were the professionals, they knew what they are doing, and all I could do was be there for him, support him in any way I could.

As they gently peeled the layers away, it became apparent that this was no ordinary breakdown over a relationship. This was serious. As they continued to probe, they asked about any other injuries or self-harming. He dodged them for a time, but after a few more questions it became apparent that the previous evening he had tried to take his own life by jumping/falling out of his barrack room window. Luckily he landed on his head, and as everybody in the RAF or RN knows, this for anyone in the Army is okay! Luckily, being so drunk when he picked himself up, he returned to his room and fell asleep, waking in the morning with just a stiff neck. But this news obviously brought an added twist, and now the medical staff were concerned about possible neck injury. Panic ensued and medics started running around, talking back boards and hospitals. The whole time, Justin was like a rabbit in headlights. I guess he felt completely out of control, and it was all I could do to stop him from fighting his way through the growing number of medics to escape. Once again he listened to me, trusted me. I don't think I really took this new information in at first. All I remember is having an overwhelming urge to put my arms around him and make it all better. I guess that was the mother in me, but I was his boss as well as his friend, and I wasn't sure how he would react to that, so I just tried to keep his as calm as possible.

Before long he was strapped to a back board and being wheeled into an ambulance, to be taken to Kings Lynn A&E. I followed behind, wondering what the hell had happened to what started out as a normal day. On arrival I quickly found where he was, though it wasn't difficult to spot the guy strapped to a stretcher in full combat uniform. He looked relieved to see me and calmed down a little. Over the next few hours of waiting we chatted, even laughed at times. They had removed his boots (can't remember why) but as he was going to X-ray I needed to go and get another car parking ticket for the vehicle, but he wouldn't let me go without taking his boots with me. There was no way he was leaving them unattended in the hospital, as he was convinced someone would steal them!

It was while we were waiting, with Justin still strapped to the stretcher, that I looked at this big strong military man and saw a frightened little boy. *What had done this to him?* I didn't know. What I did know was that he came back a little when we talked, relaxed a little when we laughed, and his eyes were asking not to be abandoned, for understanding, for help. I had no experience of anything like this but he was a friend and I could help, I could be there if he needed me, and we could do this together. It wasn't a conscious decision on my part, but I guess it was a decision I made.

He was eventually released from hospital with no neck or back issues, luckily, and even though they were concerns about his mental state they agreed to release him to my care. I have been caring for him ever since. Over the next couple of weeks he had a lot of setbacks, but each time we worked through them together. I would even insist he stayed overnight if I was worried about him. In fact, I was so worried about him one night that I made him sleep in my bed with me. At that point he was in no fit state to argue with me. He had begged me to take him to be admitted, but my gut instinct was that that would only make things worse, as his worst fear was being locked up again (he had been sectioned while still in Germany). To me, keeping him close was the only way I could ensure he was safe. We find it funny now, but at the time I didn't know what else to do.

Several weeks later, one evening over a glass of wine (or maybe a bottle), Justin made the first move, and to my complete surprise I realised I felt the same way about him. Neither of us had been looking for a relationship. We had both been hurt previously and I was acutely aware of what another breakup could do to Justin if it didn't work. What if he wasn't thinking clearly and would regret it later? I didn't want him to think he was obliged to stay with me because I had looked after him in his hour of need. Well, if you are going to jump in, do it with both feet I say, so I did. I knew instantly that he was the man for me, for as long as he would have me. I was a Nanny and I had bagged myself a hunky soldier boy! He was subsequently diagnosed with severe PTSD brought on by numerous operational tours to Bosnia, Kosova and Iraq, and discharged from the Army less than a year later.

Looking back, it was that day that changed both our lives and I have no regrets at reaching out that hand of friendship. Little did we know that within six months of that day I would have requested to leave my career of twenty-eight years in the RAF in order to become his full time carer. Within twelve months we would both have left military service, and bought our own house. We got married on the 16th January 2015, just over three years from when we first met. We've now moved to Newark, into what we hope will be our forever home.

Justin and I talk a lot about his PTSD and how he is feeling. Although he never talks about specific incidents, you do get a feel for the terrible effects his particular experiences have had on him. Before that day I had no idea he had tried to take his life on several other occasions. I didn't know that the stress of keeping it all hidden had probably resulted in the three major and four minor heart attacks he had suffered, as well as the minor stoke. How he suffered panic attacks in crowded places or couldn't sleep due to nightmares nearly every night, how certain sounds or smells gave him flashbacks, or a news event would rekindle memories he would rather forget. He had been suffering in silence.

Sometimes it's hard being on the sidelines when caring for someone with PTSD. You're both in the same place, seeing, hearing, and smelling the same things, but having two different reactions. The things you used to enjoy are no longer enjoyable because the person you want to share them, with can't. For instance, I love fireworks but I've seen first-hand what they do to a PTSD sufferer. You just have to be there for them though, support them in whatever course of action it is they need to take to ease the difficult feelings. It's all about support; they need to know you are with them, that they are not alone.

Life may not be easy for us, but we are happy and laugh a lot. We have up days and down days, but PTSD can be a bitch like that, you never know what it will do next or when it will strike. You can try and brace yourself against events you know might be unsettling, and avoid known triggers, but as much as you try it can still catch you off guard at times. It's no wonder this illness has baffled doctors for decades, because no two sufferers have the same symptoms. In Justin's case, as well as the usual symptoms, he also suffers from chronic muscle and joint pain in his legs, a common symptom of PTSD which now forces him to use a wheelchair or mobility scooter when required to walk any distance. It's hugely frustrating for a young (ish) man who was so physically fit, and thrived on pushing his body to its maximum during training. But this is what we live with, and we muddle our way through, often telling ourselves that we are what we have experienced; it has made us who we are, and in a strange way we are together because of it.

A Mother's and Wife's Love
By A Soldier

My story starts in the middle of the training area in the north of Germany. I was on an exercise in a defensive position, stuck in a trench, cleaning my weapon, and waiting for new orders. Suddenly my corporal called out, "SMITH, report to Company headquarters, now." Instant fear overtook me. What was going on?

I made my way to Company headquarters. My mind was a swirl of fear and curiosity. On arriving, I was met with surprising kindness by our Adjutant, who explained that the Military Police were there to take me back to our camp in Munster, where I was to change out of my military clothes into my civvies, and be taken to the Airport. My mother, who was suffering from cancer, was gravely ill. My father had phoned camp and asked if I could come home. At that time, as a young man, I didn't realise the implications of what was happening or why. Everything was a complete roller coaster. I had no idea, no control, and no real understanding of what was happening.

I arrived at Heathrow airport and was met by the police, who whisked me off to Birmingham. I remember changing police cars on the way and I finally arrived at Queens Medical Hospital, Selly Oak. I cannot describe how I felt when I saw my Mother in the hospital, except to say it was pure joy. I knew she wasn't well, but didn't realise how poorly she was. I was just glad to see her. Little did I know it would be the last time I saw her alive.

For a couple of years after my mother's death, I was in a very bad place. I struggled with how God had let me down, taken the only person I had loved and who had loved me back, regardless of my misbehaviour. For a long time after my mother's death, I was very, very bitter that I hadn't had the chance to show her how much I adored, missed and loved her.

I became an angry young man; my behaviour for some years after my mother's death was very poor, in particular to people who loved me. But time heals, and I then met my wife, who became my rock. Her patience and love got me back to being a normal person, minus the anger. During this period of anger the military were very good to me and stood by me throughout.

My Beginning

I was born in 1944. I believe I was what was known as a War Baby. I was taken in and looked after by nuns, who were from the Saint Joseph Roman Catholic Organisation. I lived in the Home for eight years, and the vast majority of my memories were happy ones, though life was tough and you had to earn your place amongst the other boys. I have to admit, I learnt many tricks, but one always seemed to pass me, and that was to have someone come to visit just me.

It is difficult to express the feeling of being lonely while living amongst other people, when in fairness most were really friendly. The nuns in particular gave a lot of their time to us boys. I guess it was the lack of feeling that you were an individual.

At seven years of age, I met someone I was instantly drawn to. Her name was Marg, and she was the younger sister of one of the nuns who looked after me. We got on like a house on fire and one year later, she and her husband adopted me. For the first time, I had my own Mum and Dad.

Life away from the Convent

The next few years were painful. Adapting to life out of the convent was, to say the least, very hard. I found myself in a class some eighteen months my junior because my education had been poor. Children can be cruel, particularly if they think you're different to them. I didn't understand at my young age that the school I went to on being adopted was Church of England. I had been brought up in a Catholic home, though, and although the nuns were very good, as teachers they lacked the necessary qualifations to teach us children, apart from religion, which I knew backwards. Entering a class some eighteen months younger than I was, as well as learning different religious beliefs, became too much for me handle. My mother, I found out later, figured out what the trouble was and got me into a Catholic School. From that time onwards my life got better, simply, I believe, because the teachers understood where I had come from and why I was so backwards in my education. Because of the teacher's actions, I became a normal young person to all the other children and became one of them.

Living with my Mum and Dad was never a problem. I loved being part of family life, meeting Grandads and Grandmas, who I thought were the wisest people I had ever met, with their stories and love. I never felt lonely again during my childhood, even though I was an only child.

Leaving School

On leaving school I worked in a couple of factories as a machinist, and then an apprentice tool setter. But I was bored and decided to join the TA 23rd SAS in Thorpe Street, (Special Air Service), Birmingham. I had a great time with them and one of them told me I was a natural-born soldier, and should join the army.

My parents fully supported my joining up. My mother said, "This is your home, now and always, and don't you ever forget us." I'll never know, but later in life, I always felt my mother knew that although I was happy, I always yearned to be part of a group.

I joined the Army, and I fitted in like a duck to water.

Meeting my wife in 1970 was another major step in my life. She taught me that love can be different, and with her patience and help I stopped being the angry person who didn't really care about work, or indeed, I'm afraid to say, what others thought of me. After getting married to my wife within three months of our first meeting, I started to get on with life in a much more positive manner.

We are still together some forty years later.

The day of the bomb

Fortunately, not many people have had the experience of a

bomb situation. It is a time when all sorts of emotions hit people; some are scared, some freeze, some run around completely at loss what to do. What has to happen, particularly in a military situation, is control. Carry out the basic action, which your training has taught you.

The day started out like any normal day in Northern Ireland in the early 1970's. Patrols went out on the streets to observe and, hopefully, allow the public to live as normal a life as they could, under the circumstances. Inside the camp we had occupied, life was normal; some people were sleeping, some were on cleaning duties, and some were on other duties. I was patrolling the camp, carrying out my morning inspections, to ensure that the camp cleanliness had been carried out to a good standard. My favourite saying if I found any dirt was, "Dirt kills. Therefore, soldier, your sloppiness leads me to believe you are trying to kill me, and I am not happy about that!"

At certain times it was our job to lock or unlock the city gates. We did this by sending out a patrol of four men, under the leadership of a corporal, every morning to open the gates, and in the evening to lock them. We had carried this duty out successfully for many days. This particular day, I suddenly heard and saw this soldier running towards me, shouting. When he got near me, I heard him shouting, "Bomb! "A bomb's gone off."

My Officer Commanding (CO), along with the senior members of the company, had discussed such a situation involving a bomb occurring and what we needed to do during our NI Training.

On receiving the news, I went and woke our Platoon Commander, who had been up most of the night and had not long gone to bed. He was one of the most professional people I had ever worked with.

The technical part of the operation was simple. We were duty platoon, which meant we were on camp cleaning duties. My platoon commander would go to the incident room and do what needed doing. My job, along with others, was to ensure everyone stayed switched on in the camp. The second-in-command of the company, another good, steady hand, took immediate control of the operations room. Most of the remaining two Platoons, along with the CO party, left the camp to go to the scene of the incident. One platoon, mine, went about immediately making the camp water tight.

You can plan and talk about given situations, but what you cannot anticipate is the reaction of the humans involved.

People were walking around as if in a dream. I seemed to move into a different gear, and bullied, shouted, or spoke softly, all without thinking about it, to make sure people stayed professional and did their duties.

Once we felt the camp was running as it should and all were carrying out their duties, we reported back to the second-in-command in the operation room, and told him all was running smoothly. At this time he briefed us about the incident. Rumours had circulated, but I never did, nor do I now, listen to rumours.

The truth, and the bottom line, was that one of our company had been killed by a bomb at the gate he was unlocking.

I have always believed that direct communication is the best way to maintain order and discipline. I immediately went and briefed the men under my control, and told them what had occurred. I had already told the soldiers to make sure that no soldier was to be on their own in the camp area.

My young platoon commander had taken over the security of the camp and was doing a great job. After a while, we felt the camp was running fairly normally, under the terrible conditions we found ourselves in.

The second-in-command called for me, and said the CO had requested further assistance at the incident scene.

I was to take some extra soldiers and join him at the incident. If I'm honest, I didn't really fancy going to the incident. However, my CO wanted me, so I led a small patrol out of camp and to the scene.

I had never seen what damage a bomb could do. Not only the physical damage, but you could feel the fear around the area as well.

I reported to the CO, who explained that the cordon had to be much larger because parts of the body were spread around a much larger area than at first thought. He was fully occupied dealing with lots of different tasks, which he needed to get done, so he explained to us what he wanted and told us to get it sorted.

One of the young officers went white during the brief

from the CO, and I thought he was going to be sick, however he recovered his composure. We discussed how and where the extended cordon was to be placed. We felt it was important that we briefed the soldiers whilst moving them and explained what was happening and why, to a degree, but didn't need to mention that people would be looking for parts of a body. Without doubt, the two young officers were superb that day.

Emotions run high in situations like this, not only from your own troops, but from the general public. Some of the things that were said to the troops were very difficult for them to listen to, but it was important they did, because failure to do so could have escalated the situation. It could have moved from a dark and dangerous situation to a violent one very quickly, which was clearly the aim of some of the public present.

From my perspective, although I only played a minor role in the events that day, I saw many people doing their jobs very well, but some needed a little help. I had total confidence in my CO and the second-in-command and other senior members of the company that day to do their jobs. They did, and their strength helped the rest of the Company fulfil its duties in a very professional manner.

Reflecting on what helped me through the bombing

My days living in the convent taught me how to survive in a group of people. How to ensure I got what I wanted, but not at the expense of other's feelings. When I left the convent, I had to learn new skills, particularly to deal with other children, who can be pretty awful without really meaning to. The behaviour that came naturally to them was completely foreign to me, but that is another story for another day.

Although I was well looked after in the home, the care and love from the nuns was shared amongst many other boys.

I learned what true love meant, which my mother gave me, and without which I wouldn't have survived during my first few years living outside the convent.

I met kindness and efficiency from the young officer, who met me that day, back at the camp in Germany; who had sorted out my journey home. His actions that day ensured I got home to see my mother before she died. I was given leave to stay at home by the Army until after my mum's funeral.

The pain of losing my Mother ran deep within me. It's hard to describe the feeling...I felt robbed by God, didn't want to talk to anyone about my mother, and I became angry, which at that time I thought eased the pain I was feeling. Throughout this period of anger, the military stood by me with patience, understanding, and firmness.

My only regret then, and to some degree still, is not having the chance to show my mother how much I had loved her. Eventually, I met and talked to a military priest who helped me understand, and showed me how to deal with the awful pain I felt losing my mother.

Everything I'd learned in my life to that time, from living in the convent, moving to my own home with a Mum and Dad, to going out on my own and joining the military, and getting married, taught me how to deal with the horror I saw that day.

Hopefully, I was able to help a few soldiers through an awful situation on that day, and other days, because of lessons I had experienced in my life. It has most certainly helped me through my life.

The love of my mother and the love of my wife gave me many skills and confidence about life. They have, without exception, helped me become the person I am today.

I still think God shows his love in some strange ways, though!

TODAY
BY RACHAEL CUMBERLAND

Today's the day. I can't believe it's finally here. I'm standing outside, waiting for the car to arrive to pick me up and it's already half an hour late. I am practically hyperventilating. I am never late! And all I can think about are the bell ringers. You see, today is my wedding day and I promised I wouldn't be late. I turn to my dad and say, "What about the bell ringers?" and he replies, "What will Nathan think?" But I'm not worried about Nathan, my Dad doesn't realise exactly what we have been through together this year, no one does. I don't need to worry about him, he knows I'm coming.

You see, less than a year ago, I didn't think this day would happen. Let me tell you the story....

That Wednesday started like any other Wednesday. I got up and got ready for work. I was really missing my boyfriend, Nathan. He had gone to Afghanistan five weeks earlier, and I was more than aware I still had another four months before I would see his face again. I couldn't let myself think about the alternatives. After all, he was in a war zone and some people weren't returning. Nathan was managing to ring me, but even these phone calls were few and far between. The last one was the early hours of Sunday morning, and we had been cut off. I was lucky, though, because I had met a lovely group of military wives and girlfriends whose partners were in Afghanistan at the same time, and we gave each other much comfort, always talking on Facebook and helping one another through the darker days.

I was a self-employed hairdresser, and this particular day I had allowed myself the afternoon off work to meet my mum in town. We were going to get some more stuff to send to Nathan. We were sending him about five packages a week. My soldier would know I was missing him!

When I was in town, I remember checking my phone for the time, and seeing two missed calls from Nathan's step mum. Odd. She usually sent me a text to see how I was doing. So I rang her back. Maybe she wanted to invite me for tea. However, I knew straight away from the tone in her voice that this wasn't about having tea.

"Where are you?"

"I'm in town, why?"

"You need to get here, now."

"Are you okay?"

"You just need to get here, now."

I cut the call and started to panic. Something was really wrong. I felt sick as I felt the fear rise within me. My mum and I rushed to Nathan's dad's house, and the first thing I remember was seeing an official looking man standing on the doorstep of their house, talking on his mobile. Oh, this was bad. I ran in the house and prayed for it to be something else. *Please don't let it be about Nathan.* No such luck. As soon as I saw his dad crying on the sofa, I knew. *Oh my God, he's dead,* I thought.

I heard someone screaming, and it wasn't until later I realised it had been me. I remember two arms grabbing hold of me before I fell, and someone telling me, "He's alive." The official man gently told me that Nathan had lost his legs, but was still alive. I remember him using the technical terms and my brain struggling to concentrate on what he was telling me. I know it didn't sink in, I just couldn't process it. The rest of that day passed in a blur of telling family and friends what had happened. However, the light for me of that day was that Nathan actually managed to phone me. He gave me hope. I now knew he was going to be okay, and I can't express the relief and gratitude that swept through me. He asked me if I still wanted to marry him, and of course, I told him to stop being silly. Doubt was never further from my mind.

I think people would assume that that was the worst day of my life so far, however, they're wrong. I accepted the news that my fiancé had lost both of his legs, and I went on auto pilot, working out how we would deal with it, what I had to do to make our lives work again. Would I need to move to Birmingham, where he was staying in hospital? What would I do for work? My mind was working at 100 miles per hour.

Two days later, Nathan was flown back to England and we finally got to see him. On arrival at the hospital, we were ushered into a room and told the full extent of Nathan's injuries. Still, it didn't really sink in, and we were taken up to his room. When I saw his face, tired and battered, I had to hold back my tears. Nathan wouldn't appreciate them. Being a military man, he needed me to be strong. They don't show strength through tears, but rather by getting on with things, so I knew that was what I must do. Those first few days in the critical care ward were by far the worst days of my life. Seeing Nathan's eyes rolling in his head because of the pain he was in, was agonizing for me. I am a fixer, a problem solver, and here I was with a problem I couldn't solve.

Then, one day I went to visit Nathan and he excitedly told me he was getting a wheel chair. I remember thinking, *but it's only been a few days*. There was nothing stopping my soldier, though! After only four weeks of being in hospital, Nathan returned home for good. I was in absolute amazement. Since then, Nathan has defied all the odds and worked harder than ever to start walking again. It's certainly not been plain sailing, and at times we've had some blooming good arguments as we learn to build a new way of life together. We've had to learn to fall in love again and again, as we've gone through these changes. The hardest thing for me is letting Nathan regain his independence. When he was first injured, my role was very clear – to take care of him. The vows I was prepared to take — "In sickness and in health" — I already took seriously, and I got my identity by looking after him. However, being a military man through and through, Nathan gradually wanted his own independence, and he would get mad if I treated him as injured, even though I was "only trying to help." I've had to relinquish my role as caretaker the stronger he has become, and that was really hard. I felt like he didn't need me anymore. Over time, though, I have come to realise it is far better to be wanted than needed.

So, here I am, walking down the aisle on my wedding day, brimming with pride as my husband walks, yes, *walks* alongside me. Yes, life has thrown some huge challenges our way, but together we are stronger than we could ever be apart, and I know that even though the future might have a few more obstacles to overcome, we will do just that. Overcome them!

My advice to anyone facing my situation is to be kind to yourself, and to seek support from those around you. You can have a great life, you may just have to change your path slightly.

Highs and Lows
By Nathan Cumberland

I'm walking along the off-road track, thinking, why am I here again? I'm hot, tired and sweaty. Did I really volunteer again for this shit? I'm missing home, wondering what everyone is up to. Missing small comforts such as cold water and fast food! I'm wondering what time I can get to the phone so I can ring my girlfriend, Rachael. I'm aware of the young guys around me and the fact that I am responsible for them, for their safety, and whether they make it home or not. You see I'm a Recce commander, in Helmand province in Afghanistan, serving proudly with the 1st Battalion Grenadier Guards. I'm on my fourth patrol of the day, and it's not even noon. Myself and the lads aren't thinking about getting shot, we're thinking about stepping on an IED – an Improvised Explosive Device. However, I'm not too concerned as we have already patrolled this area for the past four days, without repercussions. I've been in Afghanistan about five weeks, and I still have a long way to go before I'm on R&R. I wonder again why I am here, although to be fair, I know I wouldn't be anywhere else than with these guys. It's a brotherhood. This being my third tour, I've seen the kinetics (i.e. fighting with the Taliban) have changed hugely, from 2006 where the IED was very rare, to 2009, where you're more worried about the IED's than getting hit by a bullet.

The next thing I know, all I can hear is ringing in my ears and there is dust everywhere.

I look down at my legs. I'm facing the opposite way from the direction I was heading. My left leg has been blown off, and my right leg is dangling, attached by a few strands of muscle. Immediately, I knew I had stepped on an IED. My first thought was to stop the blood flow, but as I prepared to try, the Taliban started firing rounds at us. Seeing rounds bounce around me, I start to shout instructions to my men to return fire, and to get me my medic. The pain is excruciating, and far worse when I attempt to tourniquet my own injuries. I'm awake throughout the whole process, and when my medic eventually arrives to inject me with morphine, he accidently injects himself in the panic. Something we laugh about now. From the explosion to ending up in a hospital bed was approximately thirty minutes, surely the longest of my life.

Waking up in hospital was the first true realisation that I had lost both of my legs, and my life would never be the same again. Now, there are two ways to tackle this problem. Route A) Let it consume you, feel sorry for yourself and give up, or route B) You can accept it and deal with the fact that the life you knew before is over, and it's time to get on with a new one. I have tried to stick with route B since the very first day. There have, however, been days where life has tested me. For example, catching MRSA, (the 'super bug' infection, resistant to antibiotics), and having the skin grafts fall off, weren't my finer moments. But through all the ups and downs, thanks to having a strong family and friend network, and the love and support of my wife, Rachael, I have been able to tackle these setbacks head-on. It's not been an easy ride, and there have been times I have wanted to give up altogether, but I look at my family and remember that I am one of the lucky ones who got to return. I owe those soldiers who lost their lives to keep facing mine, and to live it to the fullest.

Together, my wife and I have made a new life, a great one, and we have been lucky enough to have been blessed with a beautiful child who is now four years old.

So, my message for anyone reading this, is that although there have been hard times, there have also been real amazing highs. I've done things I would never have dreamt of doing before this. I have truly learnt that life is fragile, and we need to live each day as if it's our last.

A PROUD MUM
BY TERESA

My son served within the Grenadiers for twelve years. He has now been discharged due to post traumatic stress disorder, or PTSD.

During his time at school, he always said he wanted to join the Army, so I supported him all the way. I remember going with him to the careers office. When he had his medical he came out and said he hadn't passed, jokingly! But then we got called into a room where they congratulated him for passing. That was a very proud day for me.

When he left to join up, I had mixed feelings, as I wasn't going to see him every day anymore. During his passing out parade, I noticed a big change in my son; he had become a grown man, and a soldier. I was the proudest mum in the world. It's so hard to see your children grow up so quickly and leave home, to say goodbye and not know when he will be home on leave again. I found it very hard to deal with, as I was worried about things like whether he was eating enough, and if he was sleeping okay. My time looking after him was taken away from me, and I had to try and accept it.

I remember the first photo he had taken in his uniform. He called me up to meet him in town, and when I got to him, he handed me the photo. I said, "Where is the bag for it?" as it was raining and not protected. I thought, that's boys for you. I still treasure that photo, and it has a special place in my home and my heart to this very day.

On one occasion, I was deeply upset with the way he was treated by the Army. He had lost a baby brother of three days old, and some time after the funeral, we found out the hospital had kept various organs from my baby without my consent, which was incredibly upsetting for the family. My son was promised time off to attend the burial of the organs, but at the last minute he was told he couldn't attend, so he went AWOL, and for a little while I didn't know where he was. He turned up a couple of days before the funeral, which was good, as I knew he was home and safe. On the day of the burial, I was worried that my son would be arrested, which put extra pressure on the day for all of us. I couldn't concentrate on the burial, because I was so concerned about the possibility of my son being arrested.

When my son returned to his camp, I rang his Officer in Charge and told him how upset I was with the way they had dealt with my son. If they make a promise, they shouldn't go back on it.

My son went on and settled well into the Army life, eventually meeting a lovely girl he later proposed to. It was nice knowing that he would settle with someone who really loved him. When my son received his posting to Iraq, he only had four weeks to arrange his wedding before going, but it all came together well and was a lovely, proud day.

Another proud moment in my life was when he had his first daughter. He was home on leave from Iraq and nearly missed the birth due to his time off running out, but luckily he was there when she was born. To see him hold his daughter for the first time was wonderful, but also incredibly heart breaking, as I knew he was going back on tour. It was then that I noticed a difference in him. He was very quiet and deep, and just wanted to be with his wife and children. I remember him getting home in the early hours of the morning and knowing he was home safe made me relax, though I never saw much of him, as he lived away, but I enjoyed talking to him. Just to hear his voice was wonderful.

He did three tours of Afghanistan and that was the worst time of my life. Watching the news 24/7, I remember the first time a grenadier got killed, I was uncontrollable. Once I got a message to say he was okay I was relieved, but felt so guilty that some other family had gotten the news no mother wants to hear. Words cannot explain how you feel, and it's something which stays with you. Because I never knew where he was, I always thought the worst was going to happen. On a few occasions, I wished he hadn't joined up, but then I thought of the time when he would be home again, and that kept me going, to a degree.

On his last tour, he told me he had a bad feeling about going back, which made me worry even more. After he had left, his youngest daughter would hear an airplane and would run into the garden and wave, shouting, "I love you daddy, bye-bye." I cried when I was told about it, and I could easily break down now thinking about it.

One time whilst he was home on leave, one of his friends was killed. The look on his face will always stay with me. I found it hard to cope with. To see your child that upset, and be unable to help, is unbearable. I worried even more when he went back out to Afghanistan. I was evil to talk to some days, and others, I would just sit and cry, wanting it to end. While he was in Afghanistan, I attended the funeral of my son's Grenadier friend. That was one of the hardest days of my life, as that could've easily been my son. But I wanted to show my respects, and be there for my son.

When he left the military, I thought it would be over, but he was having problems. He was diagnosed with PTSD. I find that hard to cope with, as I never know what mood he is in. But I'm there for him, and will always be there for him. I will be forever proud of him. He went from a boy to a man in such a short time. I blame the Army for the way he is today. I don't think the guys receive the support they deserve. The authorities just wipe their hands of them after they're out. It makes me very angry and sad.

I am thankful to the Newark Patriotic Fund for the help they have given me, as parents have no one to turn to, and I feel that I am one of the lucky ones to have the support from this group.

The Tenor Bells
By Jarra Brown

Church bells are synonymous with middle England; of quiet market towns, leafy hamlets and sleepy villages. They have represented the start of new lives, new unions, calls to arms, and national celebrations.

But when I hear church bells, I think of the fallen—the 345 people—342 men and three women—who passed through beautiful rural Wiltshire into Oxfordshire, not hiking across its pastures, or on the number 55 bus, but in a 2ft x 6ft box, cloaked in the colours of our nation.

By the end of August 2011, the bells of St Bartholomew's Church in Wootton Bassett had tolled more times than I cared to think about, each chime representing the moment the police convoy accompanying a hearse from RAF Lyneham entered the town's High Street.

Heads bowed, the chatter of curious children was quietly hushed, and gentlemen old enough to remember the conflict of 1939 to 1945, would remove their caps—those who could, pulling themselves out of their wheelchairs to pay their respects, standing smartly to attention.

It was a moment frozen in time, and the remarkable thing was that it wasn't orchestrated, it wasn't choreographed. There was no call to arms by the town crier. It was spontaneous, modest, unprompted respect.

It was a chapter in my life I can never forget. A mixture of deep sadness, chest-swelling pride, and so many mixed emotions.

And it was those remarkable scenes that I witnessed over four and a half years that compounded me to record my memories in a book I had published called, "46 Miles".

But let me rewind.

I was a local village policeman, serving with a neighbourhood policing team in a relatively unknown area of

North Wiltshire, called Wootton Bassett. It was at the end of March 2007 when I received a call to attend the local RAF Base, RAF Lyneham.

And this is how my story first started.

The Station Commander of RAF Lyneham requested my presence at the final rehearsal of a military ceremony, for military personnel killed in military operations who had returned home under the operation order, Op Pabbay.

I have emphasised the word military several times to give you a feeling of the confusion I felt when I was invited; I was a civilian police officer, so I pondered why I was asked to attend.

What I witnessed, though, was the most honourable ceremony imaginable. The last post sounded as the bearer party carried a Union flag draped coffin off the aircraft to the waiting hearse. The attention to detail was incredible; they even had actors portraying the part of a bereaved family, and the drills were immaculate, true military precision. It was a surreal experience, one that provoked significant emotion, due in particular to being a former British soldier myself, and having carried two of my comrades to their graves.

I was in awe of what I witnessed, and at the conclusion, I was approached by the funeral director, who made one small request:

"Officer, after the ceremony we have to convey the fallen to the John Radcliffe Hospital in Oxford. To assist us, could you escort us up to the M4?"

It was a distance of eight miles, and without hesitation I gave a positive reply. I mean, who would notice a couple of police cars, one front, the other at the rear, escorting the cortege like an abnormal load, to show a bit of respect.

And from that simple gesture was the foundation of what took place at the town. The whole country now knows it as, "Royal Wootton Bassett".

What I hadn't realised before we commenced this operation was that over 180 British forces fatalities had already returned in wooden boxes, mostly from the conflicts of Iraq and Afghanistan, after they were flown home to RAF Brize Norton. Sadly, it was only five days following the rehearsal that I received the very first phone call from a representative from RAF Lyneham.

"Bitter news, Jarra. A soldier has been killed in Iraq. Can you prepare for Op Pabbay?" By the end of that Monday, the number had risen to two.

It was on April 5th, 2007 when Rifleman Aaron Lincoln and Kingsman Danny Wilson were the first of the 345 we escorted home.

The simple gesture of escorting the cortege from RAF Lyneham to the M4 and through Wootton Bassett was noted, when an obstruction in the road brought the hearses to a halt adjacent to the war memorial on the High Street.

The spontaneous reaction of a few people, who just happened to be standing there, was to bow their heads when they saw the two Union flag draped coffins. That mark of respect was the catalyst to what evolved.

So many scenes like this were repeated, and were eventually witnessed by many, when the media focused on the respect being shown to fallen military personnel on the little market town High Street. So many images float through my head as I write this; a tsunami of devastation, the raw grief, and yet amongst it, the pride in our forces. These will be my own personal memories of those four and a half years.

This is an honest reflection of what endured when a small community led our nation into recognising our Nations armed forces, and realised our fallen deserved better than being brought home surreptitiously.

Those spontaneous actions that took place, some by fate and some orchestrated, were all with the common purpose of people wanting to do the right thing, at the right time, for the right person, our Great British hero.

There was no fabrication or manufacturing of the respect that was shown. Long before the media came along, the foundations were there. People cared, and stopped just for that brief passage of time, bowing their heads as veterans stood in the salute.

Some four years down the line, since we completed our duties and commitments in relation to the repatriations, I published a book about the whole experience.

It was a daunting experience, to put on public display such a sensitive story, but one I felt needed to be shared. I wanted to create a fitting tribute in memory of the fallen, to show their families years on that we haven't forgotten and time will not diminish their sacrifice.

Did I care too much? Was that why the sadness always followed me? I truly don't know, but camouflage was a skill I picked up in my young Commando days, so my deflection was to smile a lot, to keep the demons away. I may have worn the Green Beret and proudly served in the police, but the scenes I witnessed also showed me I wasn't made of wood.

So many times during those 168 repatriations, we would witness emotions that were so raw, so heart breaking. I tell you, it was difficult to distance yourself from that wailing, that outcry of despair, when a loved one was carried off the C17 Globemaster aircraft and we escorted them through Wootton Bassett High Street.

Even though, on the whole, the country was opposed to both conflicts in Iraq and Afghanistan, the public recognised the true cost of war, and valued our forces regardless.
The country appeared to follow the lead the small community in North Wiltshire started, and rallied behind the troops, dismissing the politics, and stood shoulder to shoulder in recognising those 345 who paid the ultimate sacrifice.

For me, there was no better sight than when I saw a homecoming parade, the flag waving, the smiles and relief as families, towns, and communities welcomed their troops back.

I was only ever present on one of those occasions. I was on duty, standing on point near the war memorial in Wootton Bassett High Street. November 2010, Armistice Day, with many hundreds once again shoulder to shoulder, at an oxymoron of a parade. The sadness was so obvious, as three days before this ceremony SAC Scott Hughes was killed on his journey home. That cloud of sadness changed as the troops marched through after their gruelling tour and the hundreds of people waiting broke into tears of happiness. Not that a war was won, but their loved one was home safe, and they proudly displayed their relief as they waved Union flags with pride.

The surge in charity events supporting our heroes was heartening and wide-spread from 2009 on. They even renamed Veterans Day, Armed Forces Day to reflect the respect for all those in the military, both retired and active.

I also felt the necessity to mention the hidden enemy, the one ignored for so many for years, but it won't go away. I realised the last three soldiers who came from IRAQ were suspected to have PTSD.

So many memories, and of course, a lot focused on that 400 metre stretch of road, the Wootton Bassett High Street, where those visions were seen by the masses.

Nothing compared to feeling the ambience created as the tenor bell tolled and the silence that followed as it rippled amongst the thousands lining the road. It really was a moment when the world stopped spinning.

It was a great honour to see those British service personal standing proud, their medals gleaming on their chests and their eyes once again witnessing mutual respect, but it was also heart wrenching seeing them breaking down to weep.

The sight of the devastation on the family's, friend's and comrade's faces as the conductor approached the war memorial, that pain, that sadness, will be a memory we can never erase. And then, the raw grief was released as the hero was brought to his resting place. Personal messages were said and flowers were laid as the Royal British Legion remained in the salute.

The hurt must be beyond comprehension for the mother who brought her child into the world, and the father is at a loss what to do as their son or daughter is carried towards them while the bugler sounds the last post. The grief of the wife, now a widow, so young and with plans of their future destroyed with the loss of her husband, or the widower who has to stand helpless as his wife is brought home in a Union flag draped coffin; children crying, being picked up to lay their flowers on their hero, but not understanding the answer when they ask, "Why, Mummy, why?" The loss for many is impossible to describe; the anger, the sadness, the emptiness, are all confusing, and the love and hurt can be seen in each of their eyes as they tell us of their pride. All this insurmountable agony as they relive that awful moment when they received that knock on the front door that took them into a new world.

A mother told me one day how she felt. "I'm going through a really hard time with it, swimming against the tide. I'm staying strong for my son, but at times it's very hard."

For some, the comfort that he is not forgotten helps them stay afloat. What becomes crystal clear is that time does not heal that broken heart, and when others say it does, they lie.

Words that were echoed far too many times by families who lost someone very special to them, tell me how, at times, it is difficult to go on.

It is for those who lost loved ones, family, and friends that I created this manuscript, in the hope it gives some small comfort that we genuinely do care.

But to finish this brief passage I make only one wish...in fact, no. I pray to God, that I never hear the tenor bell toll again, as another soldier comes home from war.

Finally Normal
By Neeve Bellringer

The day my dad was injured in Afghanistan I was packing for a week long school trip to Wales. I remember being quite excited for it and in a relatively good mood. My mother was in the living room, doing the ironing and watching Hollyoaks. My brother, Harry, was upstairs playing with his toys. The sun was out and it had just stopped raining, so when the doorbell rang I ran down stairs eagerly to answer it, so I could go out to play.

Only, when I answered it, it wasn't my friends as I anticipated. Two stern looking people wearing dark clothes stood on my doorstep instead. They didn't have to ask me to get my mum, since I usually get mum or dad anyway when somebody I don't know is at the doorstep, (even now at the age of seventeen). My mother most likely heard the stern looking people talking to me, because as I went to open the living room door to get her she came through anyhow. She invited them into the living room to sit down, but wouldn't let me enter and told me to go up to my room. Me, being curious, sat by the vent with Harry, who had emerged from his room to find out who was visiting us. We tried to listen to the conversation between our mother and these stern looking people. However, we couldn't hear anything but murmurs and decided it wasn't very polite to be listening in anyway. Mum and Dad wouldn't be happy with us if they knew we were doing it, so instead we sat at the top of the stairs and waited for mum to invite us in, or come out and tell us what was happening.

After a while of waiting, we heard my mother scream strangely. The scream was like a scream, a gasp, and a wail all in one, and was like nothing I had ever heard before and since. It was that moment when we knew there was something wrong. I took Harry back to his room and played with him until Mum was ready to call us down. When we were finally called down we weren't told what had happened, we were taken to Lisa's house by Angie, my mother's friend and stayed there until we were allowed home. I felt frustrated, confused and a bit annoyed that mum didn't tell me anything about what was going on. I was her eldest child, and it always felt like mum told me parts of things I perhaps shouldn't know, as if I was her friend as well as her daughter. It felt a bit like when you best friend tells everyone in the playground a secret, and no one tells you. I felt restless, too. I paced around one of the bedrooms, mumbling to myself and trying to remember to breathe.

By then I had cottoned on to what had happened, and thought that I had killed my own father. Every night my dad was in Afghanistan I wished that he would come home, and now, in some awful twist of fate, my wish had actually come true and he would finally come home. But in a coffin.

***

The next morning, I woke at six a.m., ready to be at school for seven-thirty, to go to Wales. As I woke up, I had to remind myself of what had happened the previous day. I only half believed it had happened, and part of me thought—hoped—it was a very vivid dream. Me and Harry both knew dad had been injured, but we had still been told hardly anything other than that. I went downstairs, ready for school, to see my Auntie Liz and Uncle Steve at the bottom of the stairs with my mum. Before I left, mum asked me three or four times if I was completely sure I wanted to go on the trip. I told her yes, and did the oh-so-cheesy, "dad would want me to," as if I was about to do something really brave and heroic. I realised I said that as if he were dead, and I had to remind myself he was still alive. Uncle Steve took me to school in his red Volvo and explained the situation to one of my teachers before saying goodbye to me and going back home to my mum and aunt.

The next thing I remember after the trip is sitting at home watching Children in Need whilst getting my eleventh birthday present early. Mum picked me up from school late evening and when we got home it was just us two. Harry and our dog, Murphy, weren't at home. When we got in, Mum sat me down and told me that Dad had lost his legs, and Harry and Murphy were in Newark with my grandma. I cried with her hugging me tightly; the kind of tight hug my mum gives when she really doesn't want us to cry. And when I calmed down a bit, she gave me my early birthday present: a blue iPod nano, which I still have sitting in my drawer, gathering dust. I stayed up until midnight that night and slept on the sofa. It didn't upset me that dad wasn't there. I can't remember any birthdays spent with my dad before then. He worked a lot and I didn't see him much so it was similar to any other birthday in that sense.

The following day we went back up to Newark, where all my family lived and still live today, so we could be closer to them and Selly Oak hospital, where my dad was. I missed three months of school, and in those three months I hardly left the house. During this time I only saw my mum, Harry, Grandma and Auntie Helen, who I lived with in my grandma's tiny two-bedroom bungalow, along with Murphy and my Grandma's dog, Muffin. I missed school, and for an eleven year old girl to be unhappy about missing three months of school, the situation had to be majorly unpleasant. And it was. My mum would be away all weekend with my dad, and she would see him in the week sometimes, too. I remember waiting by Grandma's living room window, waiting for my mum to come back. I recall feeling frustrated, too: I needed my mum, but I also understood that my dad needed her more. Mum didn't let us see Dad. I don't think the hospital would have either, since none of my aunts could see him (except Auntie Liz, if she was with my mum) and Nannie and Grandad were the only other relatives allowed in. Mum still say she wouldn't have let us see him, because of all the tubes coming out of him and the bags sucking the gunk out. Mum says that even then the doctors didn't really know which body part was which, and that Dad still has pieces of shrapnel in him. My brother didn't know anything, but eventually my mum told him that Dad lost his legs. I felt like my mum was apprehensive to tell Harry. He was only seven when my mum told him about the accident, but I kept asking when Harry was going to know, which probably persuaded her to tell him.

Finally, after Christmas, my dad woke up from his six week coma and Mum decided we were allowed to see him. When I first saw my dad in the hospital bed, he was so skinny. He had a metal cage around his pelvis to keep it together, and pipes coming out his nose. He opened his arms to me and seemed to be overwhelmed by seeing us, as his eyes were welling up. I remember how happy and excited he was. If I'm going to be perfectly honest, I only went over to hug my dad because I didn't want to offend him—I was happy that he was alive, of course. I love my dad, but I was also so scared. He was the same man and a different man at the same time, and I didn't know what to think. I slowly walked over and hugged him; it felt like Dad wouldn't let go of me. Just like Dad, I was overwhelmed. The hospital was bright and clean, but littered with broken men, most of them missing arms or legs or both. There was a weird smell in the air, which I could only assume was the smell of war wounds. The only thing I can't remember clearly from that night was whether I cried or not. If you know me, you know I cry a lot. I cry at school, at work, when I watch sad films (I still cry when I watch Marley and Me) and I secretly cry when people die on soap operas. But when I was in a situation where I was should have cried and needed to cry, I either couldn't, or didn't.

We moved to some apartments across the street, and saw my dad every evening. Before we left the flat we had to share it with a man whose relative was in the same hospital, which my mum wasn't very keen on. We were enrolled in a Catholic school: Harry with the infants and me with the juniors. While I was at Catholic school I made friends with a red headed girl named Anna, and a short Hindu girl whose name I've forgotten. They were the best friends I had at the time, and helped me forget about the past few months for a few hours while I was there. However, overall, I was still unhappy there. One particular memory is of a boy named Adam, who told me my dad deserved to be blown up. I screamed in his face, then stormed out the classroom. I was later scolded, while he got away with it. His friends had backed him up and said that he didn't say anything to me, apparently. This obviously made me hate being in Birmingham, and hate being at Catholic school even more I already had.

It seemed we did more praying than learning at school, and most students were working toward confirmation, but since I wasn't christened, I wasn't going to be confirmed. I still had to do the confirmation work though, just like the Muslim, Hindu, Sikh, and atheist children did. If you asked me now, I would consider myself religious. I wouldn't get baptised though, I'd be too embarrassed. Which is ironic, since I'm writing this as part of a book which is going to be public. I feel like what's happen has happened for a reason. Even though it was a horrible thing, and we had to suffer, some good still came out of it. I met my Auntie Jackie and my cousin Marie, my family became closer, and I think the past six years have helped shape how I am today (ugh, that sounds cheesy). Anyway, sometimes you have to go through a bad thing for your life to improve.

Eventually, we had to leave the flat we were living in, and we ended up living in a hotel for three weeks until we could finally go home. When we were home, we went back to our old school and I had my old friends back. Things went back to normal. I know they went back to normal, because I can't remember much, nothing stands out. Things were still different, too, though. I think everybody on the camp must have known about my dad, because I remember being told off for playing in the tennis courts by one of my dad's bosses, and when I said our last name was Bellringer, he started being kinder and sympathetic to us and left us alone. He sounded almost apologetic. Not everyone was nice about it, though. Like in Catholic school, the school we were in now had an Adam, too.

Things were pretty much back to normal—at least at school, anyway. It still felt gloomy and slightly stressed at home. Dad lived in the living room in a hospital bed, and things revolved around him. This was the first time Mum had to do her normal Mum jobs, along with the new nurse/carer jobs she had to do to look after Dad, so her workload was doubled. We were rehearsing for the year six leaver's play, "Oliver!", and as usual I was in the chorus. We had just finished rehearsing a dance number and we were all lying on the stage in a circle. The year six teachers and the director had turned their backs for a moment to discuss something, when Callum, a small boy with a face like a smacked bottom, started bullying another kid in the chorus.

"Why do you have to be such a horrible person?" I asked him as he taunted our classmate.

"Why did your dad have to go and get himself blown up?"

he retorted nastily.

I shot up quickly and chased him, and I knew as soon as I got hold of the runt I would give him a punch and teach him a lesson. I found it offensive how disrespectful he could be after everything my dad went though. He should be grateful! I chased him round the hall and we were just about to enter the year six area when Ms Hazeldine grabbed me and Mr. Lloyd grabbed Callum. Ms Hazeldine shoved me into the empty head teacher's office. She left me alone in there with my friend Rhiannon, who calmed me down and spoke to me until Ms Hazeldine came into the room to "talk" to me. It was halfway between consoling and a scolding.

I felt ignored at home, since all the attention was directed towards Dad. I was used to Harry coming before me, but Dad was hardly home before the accident, and then suddenly he's here 24/7 and needs all the attention. I needed to adjust quickly, which being from an army family, should have been easy.

I had auditioned for Nancy, but I chickened out last minute, and couldn't bring myself to sing in front of the man directing the play. Rhiannon ended up getting the part and shared it with Lauren (who played the part perfectly). I was left in the chorus and eventually got the part of the shopkeeper, which was a bad idea since, even though I was overjoyed to have a part, I wasn't very good at it and I was terrified. I felt like an idiot miming in the back ground, and I could hardly say my lines. Even though my confidence has significantly improved, I haven't had a main part since!

Now, six years later, things are pretty much back to normal. I'm a year twelve at sixth form, studying for A-levels. I want to be a teacher now, not a West End actress anymore, which I think Dad prefers. Plus, it's much easier to be a teacher. Dad is at home more, but still has to go to Headley Court, which is nice because I see Dad more than I used to, but we all get a break from him, too. Without a break from Dad, I feel frustrated. All the attention goes to him, but it isn't as bad as it was in the beginning. And there's the petty things too: having to watch what Dad watches on the telly, even though it's only him who likes the TV program, the lectures and talks about school, getting a job, driving. I know he means well, but it's still annoying. I'm probably just not used to the "normal" father/daughter relationship that everyone else has with their dads. The biggest difference between before and after the accident isn't the injuries or our lifestyle, though. I barely remember Dad with legs, and Harry can't remember Dad before the accident at all. It's the relationship between us and Dad. With things like this you don't cope, really, you just get on with it. I was able to distract myself by helping my mum, telling Harry and myself we had to do certain things or act certain ways to help Mum, because she already has enough on her plate. It never ends, you just get used to the way your life is now. I know that isn't very encouraging, but it's honest. I guess it's all part of being in an army family. You always have the same risks; you're never going to live in the same place and go to the same primary school and secondary school all your life, and you're never going have a normal childhood. Your parent could come home injured. These things used to frustrate me. I was never like the other kids and it made it worse when Dad lost his legs. I wasn't just a girl from an army family anymore, I was also a girl with a disabled dad. I yearned to be normal.

And, years later, I finally feel like after trying so hard to be normal, I finally am.

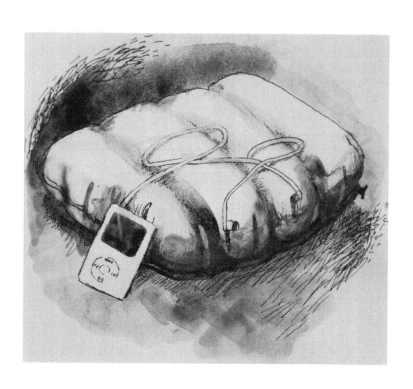

REBORN DAY
BY KEN BELLRINGER

I write this on the anniversary of my reborn day, that day, 15th November 2009, when I sustained injuries that changed my life forever.

I was one of several high threat operators deployed to Helmand Province in Afghanistan. Our job was to render safe the improvised explosive devices – IEDs – planted by the Taliban to attack British forces and other members of ISAF. This was my fourth month in the province and I had rendered safe over fifty IEDs by that point. To say I is a little unfair, as I was part of a team comprising a search element of seven, and a disposal element of four. Ultimately though, it is the high threat operator's job to take the long walk to the device, whilst everyone else stays a safe distance.

I never wanted to join the Army. Like many young boys, I wanted to be a fighter pilot. I applied to the RAF and was turned down, though I got a little further with the Navy, but failed at the Admiralty Interview Board. I was just too immature to be an officer in either service at that time. Fortunately for me, the Army flew helicopters and fortunately for me, you didn't have to be an officer. Sergeants could fly, so the Army would have to do. I applied to join the Army Air Corps, but the recruiting Sergeant informed me the quickest way to that magical third tape was by becoming an Ammunition Technician. The job intrigued me, especially the bomb disposal aspect, for I harboured a guilty secret; I thought of myself as a coward.

As a child with the surname of Bellringer, I was always going to be singled out for name calling by other children, and my angry reaction also sealed my fate, as it just encouraged the name calling. The trouble was, as much as I would get angry and I would try to back it up, I couldn't punch my way out of a paper bag. I tried, but usually ended worse off. This brought me to the attention of the bullies, and at first I just took the beating, then I started to run away or sneak about, avoiding them, and this is what I was most ashamed of.

That day in November we were located at Forward Operating Base (FOB) Price in preparation to support the Danish Battlegroup on a planned operation the following day. Morale was high, the team had established itself in Afghanistan, having undertaken many tasks without injury and only the odd firefight, which was par for the course in Afghanistan. We all enjoyed working with the Danes, who were extremely professional, and Price was one of the best places to be located for the food and welfare facilities of internet and phone access.

The loudspeaker system let out a high pitch squeal immediately prior to demanding my presence in the Ops room. I put my cards down, quite happy to be out of that particular round of the card game 'shithead', grabbed my beret, and proceeded to the Ops room. The battle captain was tasking me to a FOB south of Price. The incumbents had received information that the Taliban had arrived in the dead of night and seeded six IEDs along a regularly patrolled track. A patrol had deployed, searched and located an IED on the track, and having confirmed its presence, they returned to the FOB and requested C-IED assistance. My call-sign, Brimstone 42, was the closest.

The battle captain gave me a wheels up time and I returned to the accommodation, knowing we had to be on the helicopter in fifty minutes. I briefed the team, sparing them the specifics such as grid references, because they didn't need to know that much information. Each man then went into his own personal preparation routine. For me, this comprised checking I was topped up with water and my equipment was complete and functional, even though I had checked it twice already that morning. I then partially stripped my rifle, pulled through the barrel with a clean flannelette, wiped the working parts with an oily piece of flannelette, then dried it with another piece of clean flannelette. This may seem pointless, however, the rifle needed oil to function, but not too much because dust and sand sticks to the oil and prevents it from functioning. Yours and other people's lives depended on it. Finally, I dressed in boots and desert combats, body armour, helmet, rifle and patrol bergan, all our equipment to do the job and live. Just in case we were not coming back to Price, this included water, rations, wash kit, spare clothing, sleeping bag and inflatable roll mat. I carried two luxury items; an iPod and an inflatable pillow. This was my second pillow of the tour, as the first had sprung a leak, so as well as losing air, it was also a major loss of morale! Each man carried between fifty and seventy kilograms of kit and equipment. I was always the last to leave the accommodation, making sure no antennas, rifles or other equipment essential to the forthcoming operation had been left behind.

Now we faced one of the negative aspects to being in Price, the walk to the helicopter landing site (HLS). Most FOBs are quite compact and usually less than one hundred meters to the HLS. At Camp Bastion, we had transport that would take us there. Price provided neither and it was at least a kilometre and a half walk to the HLS. At least the weather had cooled slightly, from the 45°C of the summer to a more manageable 30°C. It was still hot, especially wearing the body armour and helmet, plus the load we were carrying, but at least it didn't feel like you were in a giant fan oven with the very life being sucked out of you. At the HLS we booked out of Price by entering our zap numbers on the outgoing sheet. The zap number is a quick identifier, each unique to the person, comprised of the first two letters of a persons surname, followed by the last four of their service number. It speeds up administration, especially in rapidly moving, confusing situations, such as a casualty evacuation or enemy contact.

Our final action was to load our weapons, and this was always done under supervision, regardless of rank. This may seem unusual for an onlooker, especially as we are talking about trained soldiers, but lives have been lost, pointlessly, due to poor weapon handling. The second set of eyes provided by the supervisor are especially useful if troops are tired or in low light conditions. Then we waited. It always seems like an eternity when waiting for transport, especially after the frenetic activity beforehand. The British Army, as with many things, has a term for it – hurry up and wait. I was always glad of the wait, because once all the preparation and checks were concluded, I could put my mind into neutral and relax. Eventually, the faint sound of the Chinook could be heard, still a long distance off, but the *wokka*

wokka sound of it's twin rotor blades as it cut through the air was unmistakable. Eventually, the large, ungainly machine came into view and within seconds was overhead, the downdraught kicking up all the dust and causing a brown out. Despite this, the pilot touched down with hardly a bump. Helicopters are at their most vulnerable on the ground, and even though we were in the relative safety of the FOB, we still had to move quickly to reduce the possibility of the Taliban launching mortar or rocket attacks that could disable a vital asset. The search advisor led the way onto the aircraft once the loadmaster waved us forward. We never ran, as any falls would take longer to sort out, but we had to shift our arses. Again, I was last. I never expected any equipment to be left behind, but checking was a good habit to get into, and it also gave me a good reason to be last on the aircraft. Being last meant I was first off, which meant I was the first to meet the incident commander, and could be quickly briefed on the situation. Being last on also meant I was near the loading ramp. I loved helicopter journeys, especially when I could look out the back. Chinooks flew low in Afghanistan, often taking sharp maneuvers, and it was thrilling watching the ground rush by. Others weren't so appreciative, fearful the helicopter would be shot down or crash, but I had every faith in the crew. Besides, the Chinook had two body guards in the shape of Apache attack helicopters ready to deal with any threats.

After a short journey, the Chinook landed and we rushed off the back as soon as the loadmaster signaled it was safe. I met the incident commander and we moved into the FOB, finally able to speak to each other without shouting as the noise of the Chinook faded away. The incident commander led me to a table and spread out a map of the area, pointing out certain features as he explained the information I'd already received, regarding the seeding of the IEDs by the Taliban. I moved into one of the sangers – guard posts – to get a real time appreciation of the ground, whilst all the time asking questions to ascertain what threat or threats faced me during the forthcoming clearance. The FOB was atop a hill west of Geresk, and at the bottom of the hill was a two to three metre wide, slow flowing stream, running from my left to my right. My side of the stream, on the right was a series of walled compounds, the usual rural Afghani's homestead, (approximately six, though it was difficult to tell as the were all linked together.) To the left was an area of scrub land, and nothing grew there, the earth was hard baked from the unrelenting Afghan sun. A track from the FOB meandered through the defensive razor wire down the hill to a narrow concrete bridge that crossed the stream. On the other side of the stream was an obvious well worn track running parallel to the stream and extending as far as I could see in both directions. This was the track seeded with IEDs. Beyond the track were irrigated fields, a metre below the level of the path, and the earth contrasted the track's pale dustiness, dark brown where it had been turned by the ox and plough team, still hard at work completing the arduous task. Beyond the fields being worked was a dense tree line.

This worried me because it was the ideal location for the Taliban to mount an ambush. I addressed my concerns to the incident commander, who assured me that the area was under constant observation, and no intelligence indicated movement in the area. The locals from the compound had been won over in the hearts and minds battle, and would inform the FOB if the Taliban moved into the area. I was still uneasy about the situation, but I had to trust the commander and get on with the business of clearing the IEDs. Following a quick brief on the plan, we moved out of the FOB, worked our way through the razor wire, and proceeded across the bridge to a small area still in line of sight of the sanger. We felt confident to do it without searching, as the area had been checked and traversed by troops, then kept under observation. It still didn't stop me from constantly scanning the ground ahead, or placing my feet in the footmarks of the man in front.

We got to the incident control point, approximately sixty metres from the marked device. I could see the white mine sticks and cylum markers through my monocular. I would go forward, alone from this point until the device was made safe. Everybody went about their business automatically; the infantry commander placed his men to cover arcs of fire and give us protection and warning of attack, the searchers set up their vallon metal detectors and tested them, my number two prepared some equipment, the bleep (Royal Signals Corporal) checked the Electronic Counter Measures, and the Weapons Intelligence Corporal passed me some gloves from the forensic kit. I briefed the Number Two on what my actions would be, took a gulp of water and after five minutes, stood up ready to make the long walk to the device. Normally, I would be encumbered with the EOD suit, weighing in excess of forty kilograms with the helmet, which offered some protection from the blast of an IED. Usually it was mandatory, however in Afghanistan, we were excused the suit due to the heat and the limitation on mobility that was incurred wearing it. I had taken a vallon from one of the searchers and gradually worked my way up the road, sweeping left to right, right to left, observing the ground I was searching, looking for the presence of the abnormal and the absence of the normal. Once tuned into the ground in Afghanistan, ground-sign was quite easy to spot and every device I found was first due to a disturbance in the earth, rather than the vallon giving any indication. The vallon was very sensitive and would indicate on any metal or magnetic source, and when an alarm was given, I would pause, kneel and fingertip search the area. Confident it was safe to proceed, I would scuff the area with my foot, to indicate a safe path for my bleep, who was following a short distance behind me carrying the ECM equipment.

Eventually, I got to a short distance from the marked area indicating the IED, and the vallon confirmed it by giving a constant high pitch squeal. I switched it off, its job done for now. Getting onto my knees I used the HD6 (a small hand held metal detector like the ones found in airports), to find the edge of the device. I moved a couple of inches back from where it indicated and scored a line in the earth. I removed my helmet, man-bag and other equipment, and placed it to one side where I could reach it, then I lay down, placing my left arm along the line I had scored. This gave me stability and was quite comfortable, so I could work quickly and constantly. Removing the paintbrush from my body armour I started to gently sweep away at the dust and dirt. Used in conjunction with the HD6 I delineated the edges of the pressure plate, working at the sides. I was looking for a wire that came from the device, often attached to a battery, allowing the Taliban to arm or disarm the device as they pleased. Neither side yielded anything, and I couldn't check the back, as that would mean working over the device. I cracked on with brushing at the front of the device, and it soon revealed a black rubber edge of the pressure plate. Underneath that, the yellow plastic edge of a palm oil container, which held the main charge, but no wire.

I needed a wire to attack, so I did what I always did, and started talking to the device, asking it to give up its secrets and make my life a little easier. For some reason I have always talked to my bombs, which isn't so bad when I'm on a real task and dealing with a device individually, but entirely different when under assessment and the instructors are there to laugh at you. It worked for me though, and here I was asking for this particular device to reveal a wire. Eventually, some white twinflex popped into view. I quickly assessed the direction the wire was going in, then gathered my kit, and after replacing my helmet I used a piece of equipment the number two had prepared earlier and returned to the ICP, making sure the bleep followed me. Once back at the ICP I informed the incident commander there would be a controlled explosion.

Once he had informed all call-signs, I gave the number two the nod, there was a small pop as he fired off the equipment, then we waited. We referred to this waiting period as a secondary soak. It's a safe waiting period that allows everything to settle following EOD action, and by varying the time, prevents me, the operator, from setting a pattern the enemy could target with a countdown timer. I took on some water while the rest of the team carried on with their business. Soak complete, I set off again, still using the vallon. I got to within a few metres of the device and assessed the results of our last action. Everything was as expected. I recovered the equipment we used and set to work on the remainder of the device, placing prussic loops on the wires and attaching them to the long line I had taken down with me, ensuring at no time did I move any part of the device whilst I was so close. Minimum time at device, maximum effect...textbook. I returned to the ICP and watched through the monocular as the line was pulled out, it popped the pressure plate, some white twinflex and the battery. After waiting for another secondary soak, I proceeded on my third manual approach, quickly checking the area where everything was pulled out. I could see the palm oil container, but nothing else that worried me. I quickly checked the pressure plate and the battery and placed them in a forensic bag and moved forward to where the device had been. All that remained was the palm oil container laying on its side with the ends of the detonator sticking out of the red cap. I taped the detonator wires for safety, but wasn't going to remove the detonator. The silvery sheen on the container indicated the main filling was ammonium nitrate and aluminium, in this case, approximately twenty kilograms. I prepared a four ounce demolition charge and laid it on the container before returning to the ICP. There was a large blast as the charge was fired, and the Taliban explosives were destroyed.

A search team usually works two abreast, covering a large area, but unfortunately this was a narrow track and we had to go in single file. The lead searcher set off, followed by the search team commander, Loren. I was third and everybody else filtered behind. We snaked down the track for about one hundred metres when the lead searcher declared he had found a device. I moved forward for confirmation and what is known in the business as a free look. Happy that it was suspicious enough to warrant my sole attention, we reversed direction along the track. Approximately fifty metres from the second device the track was wider and formed an obvious entrance to the field a metre below it. Normally, we avoid obvious entrances, but as we had the capability and were here to deal with devices, I elected the field as the new ICP. It was a little closer than I would have liked to have been, but it was also out of line of sight of the device and wouldn't leave everyone exposed on the track. The lead searcher started to search his way down the embankment into the field. He dropped out of sight from our side of the track and Loren, who's job it was to ensure searching was correct, took a couple of steps forward, but stayed on the hard beaten track; then he stumbled into the ground.

He appealed for help; he was stuck and couldn't move his feet. This was a really bad situation. Loren was stuck in a hole, a hole that had been dug into the concrete surface of the track, and there was only one reason people dug such holes. Loren stood on an IED that had not functioned, but the state of that IED had been altered, and we didn't know how long we had.

Despite all the years of training a high threat operator has to go through, and despite the experience they may gain along the way, or all the talks and discussion of previous incidents, nothing can prepare you for that moment. I can't remember thinking, but acted instinctively. We had to get out of there, but Loren couldn't move and I wasn't going to leave him. Loren didn't even know he was standing on a device, and that was a good thing, I needed him to do exactly as I said, without panicking, if we were to stand any chance. I should have shouted a warning to the others, but I didn't. It's all very easy in hind sight, of course. My focus was Loren. I wasn't scared, I had reconciled myself with death long ago and besides, this was going to work or I wouldn't be doing it, and there was no time to plan or do anything else. I don't think I thought any of what I have just written, but it's why I acted the way I did. I grabbed Loren under the elbows, with a smile called him a clumsy cunt, and tried to heave him out of the hole. Suddenly everything turned Hollywood.

Time slowed. A long, low growling boom filled my ears, followed by a continuous high pitch tone. I was lifted by the blast wave, surprised that I didn't feel any heat or pain. I seemed to hang in the air for an age and remember thinking, "this is going to hurt when I land." My eyes were screwed shut and I hit the ground hard. It felt like the back plate of my body armour was attempting to push through me and as a result, all the air from my lungs was forced out. My ears were ringing, my eyes still shut, my hands were up and out to my sides, like a baby on its back, and I didn't even consider trying to move.

I knew I was in a bad way, and all I could shout out was, "I'm still here, I'm still here." I sensed someone beside me and asked them to remove my helmet, because it had slipped off my head and the chin strap was now across my throat, throttling me. I must have blacked out, as the next thing I remember is more people around me, someone was shouting my name, and all I could respond with is "I'm still here," out of the fear they would think I was a lost cause and leave me there. I was in and out of consciousness, only responding if my name was called.

I remember being on the stretcher and being carried up the hill. The lads were running, encouraging themselves to run that little harder whilst carrying me. As time blurred together the wonderful Chinook could be heard. I sensed lots of activity, but I still had my eyes shut. The noise, heat and downwash from the helicopter was welcome, but overpowering, I heard people speaking, but didn't know what they were saying, so I just shouted, "I'm still here" again and again. Someone placed their hands on either side of my head and a female voice said, "We've got you." I went to sleep, I don't know if it's because I felt safe and could relax or they'd just hit me with a large amount of drugs. Either way, I didn't wake up for five weeks.

After battling my injuries and infection, I took the 10% chance of survival they gave me and a further twenty-one weeks in hospital, before moving on to rehabilitation.

That day changed my life forever. I've lost limbs and damaged my body to such an extent I can no longer enjoy many of the things I could whilst fit and healthy, but life isn't about what you can't do, it's about what you can do. I'm still in rehabilitation six years later, such is the extent of my injuries.

But I'm still here.

FINDING THE HUMOUR
BY KEITH

In the late seventies, my regiment was posted to Cyprus with the United Nations and my company Number One Company Grenadier Guards was posted on the Green Line to the "Box Factory." It was called the Box Factory because it used to manufacture boxes for the oranges in the groves nearby. They were the wooded, slatted kind and there were still hundreds, probably thousands, of them stacked ten feet high outside in a yard. The area had long been abandoned.

At the time I was a Lance Sergeant and I don't think my Company Sergeant Major (CSM) particularly liked me, because I kept getting all the crap jobs. We had been there about a month when he called me to his office and told me he wanted me to burn all the boxes so that the space could be used for drill practice. In reality, it would have taken me about six months to burn all the boxes, and I was fed up with him giving me all these tasks, so I hatched a plan. Now, I know I could have delegated the task to some of my men, but I decided to sort it out myself in such a way that hopefully he would stop giving me all the crap jobs. On reflection, it wasn't my finest plan.

So, petrol can in hand, I proceeded to soak said boxes and then set them alight, though I didn't expect what happened next. The boxes practically exploded, and burning chards of wood started drifting out of the yard into the nearby fields, which being dry, also burst into flames. The communication wire going to the watch towers melted and before I knew it, the fire brigade were there from both the Turk and the Greek sides, some of them not having seen each other for years. Whilst they were busy putting the fire out, a local farmer was waving his arms in the air, shouting in Greek Cypriot. The firemen knew what he was saying. He pointed out that the field was a mine field from the occupation, so everyone had to evacuate as quickly as possible. The fire burnt itself out, although there was definitely concern the fire could set off the mines.

Needless to say, I wasn't very popular and was threatened with being charged with all sorts. However, I pointed out to the CSM that all I did was follow his orders to the letter, a point he wasn't happy about. He must have spent hours reading the Queens Rules and Regulations, but couldn't find anything to charge me with. All he could do was shout at me a lot, at every opportunity, and make sure I was on duty Christmas Day, Boxing Day, New Year's Eve, and New Year's day.

Now, what happened on New Year's Day is another story, which he also came to regret...

As a result of my exploits with the orange boxes, I found myself as the senior NCO on duty at the Box Factory, whilst all the officers and sergeants mess members were elsewhere, celebrating the New Year. On the morning of the 1st January, I was busy making sure everyone was doing their jobs properly. I got a call from the watchtower that a convoy of tanks, armoured vehicles and troop trucks was coming down the road from the Turkish side. Now, being there as a United Nations unit, our role was only to observe, and not to become involved in any action.

However, the Grenadier in me took over, so I went out to the barrier, and stood there in the middle of the road with my hand raised, indicating for the convoy to stop. A rather irate officer climbed down from his tank and started to shout at me, waving his arms. Not speaking Turkish, I had no idea what he was saying, but I got the idea he wasn't best pleased. He did, however, understand what I said to him, because he subsequently got back in his tank and tuned the convoy round. I suspect they were going to drive up to the Greek's barrier as a show of force, and then turn around, but we will never know. It did, however, cause a bit of an international incident and everyone, from me to the Commanding Officer, got a bit of a bollocking.

Being in a combat infantry regiment is the most rewarding career you can have. It isn't a job, though, it's a lifestyle. Even in the most difficult of times, i.e. combat, funny things happen and sometimes you can't help but laugh. I loved my service and would not have changed it for the world.

With Special Thanks To:

Nathan and Harry Cumberland, the cover models

The Arts Council England

Supported by
**ARTS COUNCIL
ENGLAND**

global words
What's Your Story?

Global Words is a social enterprise which provides an all-encompassing service for all writers, ranging from basic proofreading to development editing, typesetting and ebook services. Global Wordsmiths, CIC is our community focused work, delivering writing projects to underserved and under-represented groups across Nottinghamshire, giving voice to the voiceless.

To learn more about our work, visit:
www.globalwords.co.uk

Other books by Global Words Press:

From Surviving to Thriving: Reclaiming Our Voices
Fractured Voices: Breaking the Silence
Don't Look Back, You're Not Going That Way
Peace by Piece
Speaking OUT: LGBTQ Youth Memoirs
Late OutBursts: LGBTQ Memoirs